Conversations with a Writing Coach

40 Conversations with Best-Selling Author
Susan May Warren

Visit our Web site at www.learnhowtowriteanovel.com for information on more resources for writers.

To receive instruction on writing or further help with writing projects via My Book Therapy's boutique fiction editing services, contact: info@mybooktherapy.com

What People Are Saying About
Susan May Warren and MyBookTherapy

SUSAN MAY WARREN DELIVERS IN CRAYON THE ALPHABET OF WRITING, MAKING GRAND PRINCIPLES ELEMENTARY. If word of mouth sells, Susie May Warren will be swamped. Since working with her I've told author friends non-stop about Book Therapy. Passionate. Funny. And knock-down-drag-out brilliant at launching my writing to another stratosphere.
~ *Jim Rubart, author Rooms*

The thorough guidance Susan Warren provides in this workbook couldn't be more simplified unless she had published it in crayon and included stickers. She transforms unattainable truth into accessible information and places it directly into your hands. The goods she delivers in the classroom in such an energetic and vivacious fashion is laid out here using the same unforgettable dance acronyms in a format that involves the writer in shaping their work in progress. No crayons required; choice of writing implement optional.
~ *L. Morgan*

POV? GMC? SOTP? Susan takes the mystery out of writing. Her enthusiastic and practical approach to teaching enlightens both novice and experienced writers. Through Susan's lectures I was able to discern a serious character Flaw in my protagonist and take that character from two dimensions to three. Her models for writing helped me make a good story, great.
~ *T. Gillespie*

Susan Warren offers a practical method of teaching that really sticks in your head. I went to a writer's conference and heard many well-known, published authors, I brought what Susan taught home to my writing.
~ *T. Stenzel*

I have taken other fiction writing workshops before, but Susan's acronyms and explanations made it click this time. Susan covered the basics (and then some) in a fun and engaging way. And I can apply this

knowledge to my project immediately. I'm confident I can write my novel now without overlooking any aspect of plot, characters or scenes.
~ M. C. Scott

Susan May Warren's class is an incredible experience which I would definitely suggest to any unpublished writers looking to get published or for beginning authors wanted to learn how to write a novel.
~ C. Fontenelle

Learning the craft of writing occurs at many different levels. Susan holds the hand of the beginning writer, explains the craft, helps him/her visualize the craft in movies and books, and most importantly, points it out in the writing of the participant.
~ R. Schmeckpeper

Susan's teaching technique is fun and fresh! Her open and honest way of communicating writing skills is highly effective. Writers of all experience levels will benefit from her creative examples of characterization and plot."
~ B.A. St. Amant

"I knew nothing about writing a novel. No experience. I didn't have a journalism degree, or journalism experience but slowly, I learned how to write a novel. More than that, SMW madebit fun and doable. My dream became real."
~ A. Wendall, aspiring author

I have read and loved all of Susan May Warren books on writing craft and this one was no different. For the beginner, It offers a solid foundation to story crafting and plan for writing your first novel. For the seasoned writer, it offers a quick, fun read that will highlight techniques that can strengthen your own stories. Her books never fail to teach me something new and push me further. Conversations with a Writing Coach would be a great resource for any writer.
~ Tari Faris, agented author with Books and Such Literary agency

I was so excited to see that Conversations with a Writing Coach contains the lessons and writing aids that took me from being an unpublished writer to published with a multi-book contract. Susan's talent for teaching the craft of writing is phenom-

enal. The lessons are easy to understand and will help beginning writers understand and develop their characters, plots and settings. And not just beginning writers—the workbook is a great refresher course for me as I begin my 5th book in two years.
~ *Patricia Bradley, author of the Logan Point series*

Bestselling novelist Susan May Warren doesn't just write award-winning books, she knows how to disseminate the process into reproducible instruction. She knows how to write a great book and more importantly for us, how to teach us to write a great book! Her lessons are practical and bite-sized. Her delivery is conversational and easy to follow. No matter what type of writer you are—plotter, pantser, or something in between—this is the book for you. It's destined to become one of the classic how-to-write books found on every digital shelf.
~ *Edie Melson, co-director Blue Ridge Mountains Christian Writers Conference and sr. editor of NovelRocket.com*

Table of Contents

From your Writing Coach

From your Writing Coach

I stink at accounting. Really. The numbers simply don't make sense to me. I'm a words girl, and the idea of putting numbers in columns in order to then read them with some understanding is parallel to the idea of speaking Klingon. But, when I started My Book Therapy, my snarl of receipts and expenses soon demanded I dive into the world of numbers and emerge with some untangled ledger.

I took a class. I failed it.

Undaunted, I took another class, this time with my adult son, who is a numbers guy. Thankfully, as the teacher assigned us lessons, my son would lean over and explain each column, help me read the numbers, and then let me attempt the answer. I started to get it right.

He explained my mistakes, told me how to fix them, and stayed the course with me, encouraging me until I got it right.

Finally, he left me alone to try and add on my own. This time, with his patience and nudging, I passed the class. (And then promptly hired him as my accountant!) Now, when he hands me P&L, General Ledger, and ROI reports, I understand them. (Basically). He cheers for me every time I ask the right questions.

This is the difference a coach makes in the pursuit of our dreams.

I am not a fan of hiring someone to "edit" an author to publication. I've always held to the idea that authors should know how to craft and wrangle a story into submission, both through structure and wordsmithing, before they submit it to a publisher. Also, using an editor in the early days of writing always carries the danger of having your Voice altered. An editor, however, is fantastic for helping after the story is crafted, smoothing it, strengthening it, and adding polish.

However, if I look back on my own journey as an author, I can distinctly see how writing mentors have come alongside me to tell me the truth about my writing and to encourage, exhort, correct, and dare me to stay the course in my journey.

This is the role of a Writing Coach. Over the past five years, I've coached hundreds of aspiring authors through one-on-one mentoring, retreats, writing conferences, online webinars, and writing-craft books. And I've seen these authors get published, win awards, and hit the best-seller list. "Sally" is the amalgamation of so many aspiring authors—smart, passionate, determined, and yet needing direction. Our Conversations are the equivalent of me cheering for you, telling you the truth, daring you to take a chance on your writing dreams, and coaching you into publication.

Maybe you like to write "by the seat of your pants," and just need guidance and a push to the next step. Or you could be a plotter, relishing that roadmap. Either way, every conversation I have with Sally will give you the direction and encouragement you need to keep going. For those who need more concrete lessons, sprinkled between many of the Conversation are Quick Skills—quick and easy lessons that dive deeper into the conversation.

Listen, there is no one right way to write a book. Although there are many different methods of putting together a novel, every person, every story is different, and although we teach a "method" at My Book Therapy (one that works!), every author has to mold that method to their own personality and style. However, the one thing we all need is someone on our side, rooting for us, willing to stay with us on the journey. Giving us the truth and daring us forward.

C'mon, let's write a book together. Grab a cup of coffee…it's time to have a conversation.

Founder, My Book Therapy

Susan May Warren

Conversation #1: So you want to be a writer

I agreed to meet Sally at the local coffee shop on a Monday morning, and I told her to bring a notebook. I'd seen her at church a few times with her four children hanging on her like she might be monkey bars. She ran the children's program and had even pulled off the church Christmas musical with twenty haloed children in under a month, so I knew she had the energy as well as the chops to realize her goal, if she wanted it enough.

She wanted to write a novel.

I told her that over the next year I would be glad to help her get all the way to a finished manuscript. She simply needed to be willing to hear the truth and dare to take my advice.

I sat there nursing my extra-tall latté, watching the snow peel from the sky, the drifts lining the rocky shoreline outside the window, and remembering my own journey, started in Siberia, Russia. Armed with just a desire to write a novel, I began to pull books off my shelves and study the masters.

Forty-five novels later, I am still amazed at the journey. I've learned a few things, made a number of mistakes, and taken a few courageous steps. And here I was, looking forward to helping Sally Anderson begin her own journey to become a published author.

She came in five minutes late, wearing a parka, a skier's hat, and carrying a messenger bag, her eyes bright, if not a little nervous. She dumped her bag on the chair and tugged out a three-ring binder. "I brought a sample of my writing," she said and handed it to me as she went to order her coffee.

I skimmed through her work while I waited. A few newsletters, short stories, a children's play, a number of devotionals. All interesting, if not just a little predictable, the writing solid, even if not engaging. I clearly recognized enough of a voice that, with the right encouragement, might sing.

She had potential. And when she sat down with her moose mocha, enthusiasm. "Thank you for meeting with me! I just love your books. I want to write like you someday."

I handed back her notebook. "I want you to write like you someday," I said with a smile. "Tell me why you want to be a writer."

I wasn't just being polite. I have found as I've taught writing across the world that there are different types of novelists. There are those who have a message and want to change the world by communicating it through a novel. These folks are zealous, but they aren't always writers—sometimes they are simply evangelists and writing a book seems the easiest way to get their message out. I fear for them, because they can become easily discouraged when they see other books written on their topic. Or, if their book, which they've worked so hard on (and which has such a great message,) is turned down by an agent.

Then there are those who have endured incredible suffering or struggles and are seeking to make sense of it through a gripping novel. Maybe, if they write a best-seller, their suffering will serve a purpose. I try to help them see the other side—the part where people might not appreciate their suffering, and in fact, the Amazon reviews might only cause more struggle (because even if there are thousands of great reviews, the few negative ones will eat away at their peace of mind). To these folks I say, "You didn't suffer so you could write a book. And your novel won't suddenly justify your struggles. You have to find that answer, that peace somewhere else." Here's some truth: If you aren't happy with who you are before you're published, you won't suddenly find inner peace after you're published. Sometimes being published can actually make that peace even a little more elusive.

So, I asked the question with a little intake of my breath, hoping...

"I think story has the power to change lives..."

Uh oh.

"I have a number of life experiences that I think would be interesting in a novel, and I think I'm supposed to share them..."

I tried not to wince.

"But really, I just can't help but write. I love words and how they flow together, and I love stories, and spend way too much time dreaming up plots. I know my kids are little, but I just can't escape this urge to write. I would do it even if I never got published."

I wanted to give her a little hug, but I didn't want to scare her off. "Yes. Isaac Asimov said, 'I'd rather write than breathe.' This is the mark of a true novelist—that idea that you can't turn off the stories or the words. You must have this kind of passion to stay the course of writing a novel, because I promise, there will come a day when you want to put the pen down and walk away."

She looked dubious.

"Your passion, however, won't let you."

She nodded.

Sally I could work with. "Do you have a story idea?" I asked, needing a warm-up on my latte.

"Not yet. Can you help me?"

"I can't help you find a story, but I can point you where to look. Every story starts with a story spark—a great idea generated by something you see or hear and nurtured by something you care about. My book *The Shadow of your Smil*, was sparked by the thought of my daughter leaving for college and what I would do if something ever happened to her. The story spark acts as your vision for your novel and generates the Story Question that will drive your reader through your story."

"A story question?"

"We'll get to that. But here's your assignment, if you dare: Write a list of five things you are passionate about. Five things you fear the most. Five things you've always wanted to do, and five interesting things that have made you stop and think in the past couple of weeks. Then apply a 'what if' question to each of those five things."

"I lost my son in the mall for twenty minutes during Christmas."

"Exactly that. What if you hadn't found him? What if someone took him? What if…I dunno…Santa took him?"

She shuddered.

"But seriously, it's those sorts of situations and questions that can lead to a novel spark. Now that you have the truth about what it takes to write a book—do you have the courage to take the dare?"

She finished her coffee and gathered her notebook. "I'm a mom. What do you think?"

Yes, I liked Sally a lot. I couldn't wait see what she'd come up with.

Truth: Novelists must have a passion for writing and storytelling.

Dare: Write your own lists of five. What Story Spark can you find?

Conversation #2: Cultivating your Story Spark with a Story Question

Snow graced our little hamlet, lacy upon the rocks of our town's shoreline, evidence of the blizzard over the weekend. A perfect opportunity to huddle into my armchair and get some writing done. Although wedged into rewrites of a story, I pried myself out to plow my way into town to meet with Sally, the aspiring writer I promised to mentor.

I hoped she'd taken my dare to dig deep into her life and interests to find a Story Spark. I probably should have told her to start an idea file. Once she started putting her ideas into a story, she'd be surprised how ideas seem to show up at all times of the day—and night. (FYI—I'd recently discovered Evernote as a way to capture all my wandering thoughts and story ideas.)

Sally found me lost in the tangle of my rewrite thoughts, nursing a skinny vanilla latte.

"Hey, Sally," I said as she unWound her scarf, setting her mocha on the table. I wanted to run my finger through all that chocolately sprinkled whipped cream.

"I think I found my Story Spark," she said as she sat down and pulled out a folder. She reached into the folder and slapped a picture down on the table. Her blue eyes shone. "The famous *New York Times* kiss picture from V-E day, 1944."

Who doesn't love that picture? The sailor dipping an unsuspecting nurse in the *Life* magazine snapshot. "I like it, but why?"

"I'm a World War II buff, I've been to New York numerous times, I am a first responder, I'm interested in medicine, but most of all..." She smiled as she drew the picture back. "I'm a terrible romantic. I know it was just a passing kiss, but my romantic heart wants to think that they had a whirlwind romance and lived happily ever after."

She'd just answered my next question without knowing it—what do you like to read? Because as she looked to put a story together, writing in a genre she already loved would boost her along the learning curve. "You read romances?" I asked, just to confirm.

She glanced around the room, lowered her voice. "I love them. Sometimes I'll read romantic suspense, but my favorite is historical romance—I have an entire bookshelf of them."

"Excellent. For the next three weeks, I want you to find your favorites and re-read them, this time to discover three things: plot, character, and story elements you love, as well as the romantic conflict between the characters and how they fall in love."

"Is that my dare for the week?" She smiled.

"No. That's your gift—you get to read for homework. Your dare is something bigger, something that will give your story real punch. Because while you've stumbled upon a fun story spark, you don't have anything original, or even sellable. What makes a story compelling and pitchable starts with something called the Story Question. It helps you create your logline, or pitch."

"Logline? Pitch?"

"We'll get to that further along the journey. For now...what is your story about?"

"True love?"

"What about true love?"

"I was thinking that the nurse could actually have lost someone in the war—maybe even a sailor. And maybe so did the man who kissed her."

"So, they knew each other?"

"Maybe they lost the same person. What if the sailor was a buddy of her fiancés, and was with him when he died—and the dying man told the sailor to take care of his fiancee. He keeps his promise, except he falls in love with her even though he realizes how terrible it is to fall for his best friend's gal—"

Yes, she had a romance writer in her. Not an elaborate plot, but a good start.

"So, the story is about second chances?"

"Or maybe second love?"

"Excellent. So, what will the story show about true love?"

She took a sip of her cocoa. "That you can lose, and love again? That it might be different, but perhaps just as good the second time around?"

I liked that theme—at least for a start. She'd discover that as she got into the story, the theme might deepen, take on nuances. It was enough to push her to—"Now, let's create a Story Question from that theme. The Story Question is the question that propels the character—and the reader — even subconsciously, through the story. It's the 'lesson' that the story teaches."

"But doesn't that preach to the world? I've read I shouldn't do that."

"A Story Question doesn't preach. It presents the question—and then explores the answers through the journey of the players in the story. The best kind of Story Question offers a few different 'answers' for the reader to consider after they put the book down. Like, is your first love always the best? Or, is loving truly worth it, even with the loss? When you start your characters out on their journey armed with this question, you allow them, and your reader, to discover the answer together."

She was taking notes.

"Try this—look at your favorite books and movies. What are some of the Story Questions embedded in them?"

"I just saw *Cowboys versus Aliens*. But I hardly think there's a Story Question there."

"Sure there is. Can a bunch of cowboys beat aliens with vastly superior technology? The answer is revealed through the movie."

"If they have enough to fight for," she said.

"Yes—which is another element we'll talk about soon—building Story Stakes. But for now, here's your truth. All stories have a Story Question, something that drives the character and the reader to discover. You'll also use this Story Question to develop the marketing materials for your book."

"Yes—they didn't even need marketing material—the title of *Cowboys versus Aliens* was enough," she said.

"You got it. Here's your homework. Figure out the Story Question of your story. Ask yourself—what is the theme of the story? What am I trying to say? What will the hero/heroine learn? And then turn that answer into a question. Bring that back to me next week, along with your very favorite book, and we'll talk about finding your Voice."

"My voice is what I use to tell my son to stop jumping on the sofa," she said, finishing her mocha. "I can't wait to use it for something else."

Truth: Every story contains at least one take-away "truth" that is learned during the character's inner journey.

Dare: What is the lesson of your character's journey? Turn it into a Story Question.

Quick Skills: Discovering your Story Question

Are you finished with your book but can't quickly articulate what it's about? Maybe you need to hone your Story Question.

The Story Question is the conscious or subconscious question that drives your character—and reader—through the book. It's the truth they are seeking to find. Or it could be the truth they will accidentally discover. Whatever it is, it's personal and something that readers themselves want answers to.

Every book, movie, and short story has a question, however subtle. The stories that ask riveting questions through the circumstances of their characters are the ones that linger with us. Consider *Of Mice and Men*. A haunting story that makes us ask—just how responsible is George for Lennie's actions? This happens to be the same question George struggles with.

How about one of my childhood favorites—Where the Red Fern Grows. Does God care about the influences and sacrifices of two hound dogs—or any pet—on a person's life? Enough to honor them with a Red Fern? Are pets sent into our lives because of some sort of divine intervention? The author explores this idea throughout the story.

That's the power of a Story Question—getting to the heart of the story, for the character, for the reader.

To discover your Story Question, start by asking, what is the overall story about? Family? Honor? Justice? Then ask: What do I want to say about the theme? What is the lesson your character(s) learns? How can you turn that around and ask a question about it? Now, make it personal and more specific.

Here's the added bonus—when you go to market the story, you'll have questions ready to raise interest. You can even use the Story Question to create a pitch: What if a fire investigator discovered that an arsonist was his brother—the brother who'd earlier saved his life?

Quick Skill: Give your story power by finding the theme, then developing a Story Question.

Would you like a free infographic and 1-hour lesson on how to build a powerful character?

Check out our Story Equation Mini-Course! *(http://novel.academy/courses/TheSEQ/)*

Conversation #3: What is Voice and how to you find yours?

Outside, the wind howled, the thermometer dropping to a bracing negative nine degrees as I waited for Sally to arrive for our Monday morning conversation. I hoped she'd found a Story Question as she thought about the theme of her story. Ironically, I'd been thinking about marketing my new book and had to return to the Story Question of that book to create the right marketing and PR campaign.

I blew on my hot cocoa, glad I'd opted for a large as Sally came in, wrapped in a scarf and hat.

Kathy already had her coffee ready. Sally set a stack of books on the table, then retrieved her coffee. I looked at her choices—*Jane Eyre*, the movies *Pearl Harbor* and *Casablanca*, and one of my favorite books—*Redeeming Love*. An interesting collection. I searched to find the connection between them as she sat down and unWound her scarf, her cheeks rosy.

"You said you wanted me to bring my favorite book."

"Tell me why you love these," I said.

"I love *Pearl Harbor* because it's a personal romance that takes place in a factual, historical context."

I nodded. "That's what makes a story set against an epic backdrop so fascinating—when it tells us how it affects individuals. James Cameron did it in *Titanic* too."

"I want to weave in the historical details, while still keeping the story focused on the character." She picked up *Redeeming Love*. "I love the theme of this one, the unconditional love of God. And the hero is so…heroic."

"So, you love the characters and the Story Question—does God love us even when our sins seem unforgiveable."

"And the way she tells it. No fancy language, just a great story." She picked up *Jane Eyre*. "And yet, I love this style of writing. Poetic and rich."

"And this one?" I held up *Casablanca*.

"The romantic angst and tragedy. "

"You are a romantic," I said. "And I'll bet a fan of Benny Goodman and Mary Jane shoes."

She nodded.

"I'm going to save our *Casablanca* discussion for next week when we talk about the four ingredients that every book has to have. But for now I want to talk to you about Voice."

The wind shook the windowpanes, a film of ice building along the sash.

"Voice is about the way you tell your story. An agent friend of mine calls Voice the author's 'Personality on the Page.'"

"But I thought an author isn't supposed to intrude into a story."

"You're correct. Author intrusion is annoying. It pulls you out of the story. It's like an 'aside' in a play, where the character walks to the front of the stage and addresses the audience directly, giving us an explanation or telling us some nifty information about the history of windmills or something the author feels we need to know, even if your character doesn't know it. This is called 'breaking the fourth wall'. It can sometimes also happen when an author wants to get on their soapbox about something, often unrelated to the plot. They just want to use their voice, now that their reader is trapped in the story, to make a point. That is the preaching you were warned about. As an author, you want to be invisible on the page. Only the characters should speak."

"Then how do you put your 'personality on the page' if you're not supposed to be visible to the reader?"

"Have you ever been in a play?"

"Actually, yes. I was a church lady in *The Best Christmas Pageant Ever.*"

"So, you know that you are given a set of lines, and you have to make them come to life. Your job is to add the life and breath to the lines. Every actor takes those lines and does something different with them.

"As a novelist, your Voice in the story is the particular way you tell the story through your characters, your syntax, your grammar, the rhythm of sentences, even your choice of words. Think of it as your 'style.'"

"How do I know what my style is?"

"Do you watch HGTV?"

"Of course."

"Why?"

"To get ideas about how I want to decorate my home."

"Ideas about what you like, right? So you'll find your style and figure out how to decorate your home with your own touches."

She nodded.

"You do the same thing with books. You gravitate towards these authors and stories because there is something about their writing and storycrafting that sings in your soul. Your job this week is to find out why. I want you to go through your favorite books with a highlighter and note every sentence, every character nuance, every plot device that you love. Even better—take a notebook and write these elements down so you can see them all at once. It's a collection of your favorite examples of Voice, and it will help you recognize the style you like."

"But I don't want to write like them."

"Really?"

"Okay, I guess I do. But my way."

"Of course. And you will. Because after you collect these examples, I want you to take a look at them and figure out why you like them. Is it the words, the turns of phrase, the rhythm, the characterization techniques? These are the things you will incorporate into your writing—in your own way."

She was looking at me like I had lobsters coming out of my ears.

"I promise, it will make sense when you do it. But before you can figure out your voice, you need to understand the fundamentals of grammar. The fact is, your Voice won't matter if you haven't nailed your grammar. The better you can write, the more your Voice is freed. Sort of like how when you know the steps of a dance, you can add embellishments."

"I have a copy of Strunk and White's *Elements of Style* at home," she said.

"Perfect. Because that's part of your homework this week. Read through *Elements of Style* and really review the foundation of properly written language. Then take a highlighter to your favorite books and passages. It's okay, it's not a sin, I promise."

She laughed. "Okay, I'll do it."

"And in the meantime, I have a test for you. Watch *Pearl Harbor* and *Casablanca* and see if you can figure out the four elements they have in common, besides the war theme. I'll give you a hint—the four things are what make a film, or a book, a best-seller."

"Popcorn, a blankie, romance, and tears?" She winked as she gathered up her bag.

Truth: Voice is an author's style...the way they tell the story. But it can only be built on a solid bedrock of fundamentals.

Dare: Create a collection of your favorite story elements: sentences, story devices, and characterization techniques to help you understand your Voice.

Quick Skills: A tip to Discovering your Voice

The concept of author Voice is so elusive, it can feel like a loose football, bouncing around the field. Just when we think we have a grip on it, it wiggles out of our hands.

Voice, in a nutshell, is your storytelling style. Words and plot and character—and how you weave these together. Much like an actor dons a role, bringing their own style to a script.

Although we can work to recognize Voice and even analyze it by finding great style in other works, we don't really discover our Voice until we put the pen to page. Until we write words that make our own hearts sing.

Here's a trick I've used to develop my Voice: Try writing the story as if you were the character. Lock yourself inside the constraints of your character's knowledge and personality—only allowing yourself to see, think, feel, and know what your character would know. Only allow dialogue that your character would say. Donned with that persona, write the story in your character's point of view, but in first person—the way you might speak. And here's the key: for this exercise…write without the rules, even grammar. You're just setting them aside for this exercise—not forever. Sometimes writing "rules" can choke out your Voice. Fear not, it's just an exercise…you'll rewrite it with all the fundamental grammar rules later. For now, just enjoy the freedom of writing without turning on the internal editor.

I've done this exercise with a number of clients—and they're always surprised at how intimate and empowered their writing becomes.

When you're finished, look for the words, the sentence rhythms and constructions, and characterization elements that you love.

This is your Voice — your style — expressed through your character and story on the page.

Of course the key to weaving that into a novel is to make sure that, although you are writing it in your Voice, you're staying within the persona of each particular character.

Once you've tried writing in first person, rewrite the section in third person. You may be surprised at how personal and powerful your Voice has become.

Note: Sometimes when I'm working on a new genre, or I'm stuck in a story where I feel my writing is tired, I try this exercise, and my Voice seems to gain a new breath and come alive in the story as I rewrite.

Fear not. Your Voice can be caught…you just have to scramble after it, land on it, and hold on.

Quick Skill: Find your Voice by writing with your internal editor turned off, in first person, and in the persona of your character.

Conversation #4: The Four Elements of a Best-Seller

I was drinking an extra-tall vanilla latte, blinking back the sand in my eyes as Sally came in. A glorious Monday morning greeted the northland — the sun winked off the frosty waves of Lake Superior, a perfect eggshell blue sky trumpeted overhead, the snow glistened under all that grandeur like diamonds.

Good thing, too, because I'd stayed up late watching both *Casablanca* and *Pearl Harbor* to prepare for our conversation this morning. I knew, after meeting with Sally for three weeks, that she took our conversations seriously, and I wanted to be on my game.

She sat down and tugged off her knitted mittens. "I started a notebook like you suggested." She pulled out a hardbound journal with a leather cover and handed it to me. I opened it and to my delight, found copied phrases and sentences, analyses of plots, and notes as to why she liked them.

"This is perfect. Have you discovered something about your Voice?"

"Yes. I love the poetry of words, how they string together, and I like to use them in unusual ways. I like stories about sacrifice and unrequited love. And I love snappy, witty dialogue. A lot of the passages I copied were examples of these."

"Excellent. Continue to study how the masters do it, and then try it yourself—in your own Voice, of course. As you get further along writing your novel, we'll talk about some tricks on how to do that. But I'm sure you're wondering when you'll get to start writing."

"But I don't even know where to start at developing my character."

"We're going to start working on him this week, I promise. You'll have homework that will help you learn the specific things you need to construct his journey. However, today I want to talk about the four elements you have to put into your book to make it a best-seller."

"I just want to get it written, first."

"But you do want it to be powerful, right? So you need to look inside the framework and produce the four elements that every reader craves. It's these four elements that draw us to movies like *Pearl Harbor* and *Casablanca*."

"Besides Humphrey Bogart and Ben Affleck?" She winked.

"They help, that's for sure." I winked back. "But if you think about both of those movies, they embody four essential plot and character elements: acts of Heroism, Sacrifice, Justice, and Redemption."

She was writing these down.

"Acts of Heroism aren't just men and women doing heroic things, like saving a child, or going to war. It's about moving your character, step-by-step, from selfishness to selflessness. You have to cause him to want the good of others by the end of the movie."

"Like Rick sending Ilsa away."

"Yes. And like Rafe wanting Danny to live at the end. And of course, Danny telling Rafe that he should raise his child. It's these elements that show us what true heroes are and make us love the characters despite their mistakes and sins.

"The second element is Acts of Sacrifice. Obviously, a hero sacrifices, and building that element into your story shows the true heroic nature of your character. It can be a sacrifice of love—like Rick in *Casablanca*—or a sacrifice of a dream—like Rafe in *Pearl Harbor*.

Or it can be a sacrifice of a friend, a job, a business. A sacrifice can be something at the end of the journey, or it might be something at the beginning of the journey, like Harry Potter losing his family before the stories open. A sacrifice makes your character just a little bit more sympathetic and likeable, and makes a reader root for them.

"The third element is Acts of Redemption. We need to see that your character, or some major player, is redeemed, and that by his actions, he has found a measure of salvation. Rick is redeemed when he discovers that Ilsa loves him and would rather stay with him. He has to 'do the thinking for both of them,' and when he does—and makes the right decision—he's redeemed from being a guy who never sticks his neck out for others. Rafe is redeemed when he loses Evelyn to Danny and realizes she will never see another sunset without thinking of him. He knows she loves him, and he is able to step away from her and let Danny have her. Redemption comes as a result of an 'Epiphany,' and helps them right the wrongs they, or others, have done to them.

"The fourth element is Acts of Justice. Human beings crave justice, and we want it in our stories. And frankly, it's why we like the endings of *Pearl Harbor* and *Casablanca*. Although Danny dies, we all know that Evelyn really belongs with Rafe, and Rafe realizes just how important Danny is in his life. This ending brings Justice to the wrongs perpetrated in the story. And Rick...he knows Ilsa doesn't belong with him, even though he has her heart. We find justice for him—and all of France—when the Prefect of Police says, 'round up all the usual suspects.' We realize that Rick is going to get away...and perhaps even get involved in fighting the war again.

"The truth is, without these four pillars supporting it, your story will be uneven, and even shaky. So, as you're creating your character this week, think about how you'll weave in Heroism, Sacrifice, Redemption, and Justice."

She finished writing. "And I suppose you're going to tell me to look for these in every book and movie I see."

I smiled. "And then write down some ideas of how you might add them to your story."

"Like losing the girl?"

"Or, since it's a World War II novel, he could lose a leg or an arm. Or a best friend. But we'll find the right Sacrifice as we build your character.

"Which brings me to a question—we haven't really spent much time on him yet."

"Good point. Yes, it's about time to think about Who is in your story. So, your homework for this week is to come up with a list of ideas for each of these elements. And then...I want you to name your character."

"Like Joe, or Butch?"

"No. Use a metaphor that captures his essence, his personality. I'll explain more about what that means in Quick Skills. But, in short, ask him how he sees himself. That will help us build his identity. And bring me a picture of your hero. I want to see what he looks like."

"Ben Affleck won't do?"

"Oh, he'll do just fine."

Truth: To build a strong story, you must have Acts of Heroism, Sacrifice, Redemption, and Justice built into the plot and characterization.

Dare: Look for these four elements in your WIP or favorite stories. Are any of the elements missing? Would they be stronger if they included all four?

Quick Skills: Who Is Your Story About? Creating the Identity of Your Character

Are you creating a new character and trying to figure out how to make him/her different from every other character you've created? Try this—instead of picking out a name from thin air and then attaching a bunch of characteristics to your paper doll, start from the inside-out.

Start with finding your character's core identity.

Identity is not about your character's career—skydiver, wilderness EMT, policeman, lawyer, photographer, chef, teacher—but rather the person on the inside that has driven them to this destiny. Often, writing teachers call this a character's essence. This essence can be an adjective, or it might be metaphorical.

Let's take a firefighter, for example. We might automatically assume he's a protector or courageous. But let's take a look at the person inside the turnout jacket. Maybe our firefighter is actually the son of the chief and the youngest brother of three other firefighters, and he's trying to prove that he can measure up to them. And, because of his experience having three older brothers, maybe he's the kind of guy who always stands back to assess the situation before running into it—a characteristic that saves lives in the end, but that makes him a poor firefighter in the eyes of others. So let's see, we can come up with words like unruffled, systematic, cautious, prudent. Once we figure out a few adjectives, let's start assigning a couple proper nouns that encapsulate his character. Analyst. Architect. Engineer. Remember, we're not looking at the profession now—we're looking at the characteristics that embody that noun.

Let's say we decide on Engineer as our character's (let's call him Hank) inner identity or essence. Although he works as a firefighter, his core essence is Engineer—which means that he embodies the characteristics of a man who considers the problem and then devises a solution before jumping in to fix it. Once we have the essential identity, we can start giving Hank other personality traits.

Perhaps he is patient. Prone to see the whole picture and not take sides. Determined to solve problems. Possibly even quiet and withdrawn as he's thinking. He's probably a pretty organized, immaculate person—at least in his private life, and maybe he's always tinkering with things, like building Tinkertoys with kids at the local daycare center where he volunteers along with the other firefighters. Or maybe he's into history, and loves researching the old buildings of Chicago (where he lives). He hates rushing into decisions, because he feels like he's going to find himself with no way out. Thus, he is super frugal and drives the same car he had in college.

It's only taken me a few minutes to really get at his essence and figure out who our firefighter really is. Now, I can build a plot around him, adding pressure points that challenge his core—like, what if he had to make a split decision and it cost lives? Or what if he were asked to take sides on something? What if someone came into his life who was a risk-taker and impulsive? What if that person was his chief?

What if the chief was a woman?

See how starting with his identity has created the start to a plot, tension, and even a romance?

Always start with your character and his core identity (and the same for your heroine), and it will jumpstart your plotting and send you on your way.

Quick Skill: Find the Core Identity of your Character, and then build the plot around that.

Conversation #5: Want to get published? Embrace Genre

Ice crusted the parking lot as I slipped my way to the coffee shop. The unusual warm spell we'd experienced over the weekend had turned frosty with the blizzard sweeping across middle America, turning the pavement to a black skating rink.

I should have expected the cold, but the sudden spell of warmth caught me off guard and ignited my hope of spring. Worse, I now nursed a cold because winter hadn't followed the rules.

Which was exactly what I was going to talk to Sally about today—following the rules as she writes her first novel.

She waited at our table, beside a crackling fire, reading her Nook.

"Hey," she said as I slid into the seat. Blessed Kathy walked over with my mug of vanilla latte.

"What are you reading?"

"A romance. Taking notes on why I like it, like you suggested."

"Perfect. Now, tell me, what do all romances have in common?"

She put down the Nook. Thought for a moment. "A hero and heroine. A common thread that pulls them together. Conflict that pushes them apart. A breakup. And a happy ending."

I pulled out a tissue. "And if you don't have one or more of those?"

"Then it's not a romance. I feel cheated as a reader."

"Exactly. You've just defined the difference between a genre novel and a literary novel. Genre novels come with expectations embedded. A mystery always has a dead body in the beginning and the goal is to find the killer. A thriller always has a catastrophe looming at the end, and what we call a "lit fuse" or ticking clock to heighten the sense of danger. A fantasy has other-world attributes that we need to understand, and women's fiction is a story about relationships and a woman's journey as she confronts an issue in her life. We expect these things when we open a genre book, and if an author tries to step out of them, instead of being considered innovative, they are simply breaking the rules."

"But aren't we supposed to be innovative? To do something unique?"

"You're supposed to give a fresh twist to the story by adding a unique plot element or character, but when it comes to genre expectations, you have to stick to the rules. Unless you're writing literary or general fiction. But even they have a standard story arc. The truth is, to be a great writer, you have to adhere to the structure of genre and story. Your innovation appears in how you deliver the story within those rules."

"Like, the Super Bowl. The Giants play the game one way, *the Patriots* another, and yet they all have to follow the rules of the sport."

"Correct. Or, think of it like a building—every building has to have a foundation, walls, a roof. The interior is where the innovation and uniqueness happen. But this works to a novelist's advantage. Instead of looking at it as confining, consider the rules as a guide to keep you headed in the right direction. When you learn story structure and then the elements of genre, you have a roadmap to developing your story. It actually becomes a sort of checklist to make sure you've created a powerful story."

"So, what is 'standard story arc'?"

"I'll give you a checklist when we get further along, but every story has the same roadmap. It starts with your character in Home World, or their status quo. Then, something happens to change this, called the Inciting Incident, which has the effect of sending your character on a figurative, or sometimes literal, journey we call the Noble Quest. During this quest, your character(s) is forced to make decisions that challenge who he is and may change him until he comes to the Black Moment—which is his worst fears coming true. At this point, he has an Epiphany, which changes him and gives him the power to do something at the end that he couldn't do at the beginning, to 'save the day.' This is the point of the story—to change your character and tell a truth through his life. Your character ends the story in a new home world, a changed person."

She picked up her Nook. "Yes. I can see how even a romance does that. My hero learns that he needs love in his life."

"Exactly. All the genre elements build on this main story arc. This week, in your reading, I want you to outline all these steps for every book or movie you read. And then, because you want to write a romance, also identify those elements that create a powerful romance. If you're looking for a resource, I have a book called *How to Write a Brilliant Romance* that also identifies and teaches you how to do this."

She pulled her folder from her bag. "And what about him, my hero? I brought a picture."

Cute Ben Affleck was pasted to the page.

"Did you give him an identity?"

"He's a healer who lost his best friend. He's besieged by guilt."

"So he's lost his confidence."

She nodded.

"Okay, that will work. Next week we'll talk about how to develop a plot around him by giving him a Dark Moment in the past. So, your homework this week is to ask him: What was the worst thing that ever happened to you? Write it down, like a journal entry. I promise, you'll use it in your story. And then, find yourself a hero-ine, and do the same."

"And in the meantime, read as many romances as I can find?" She put her Nook away. "My family may never eat again."

Truth: Genre writing is about expectations. Fulfill the expectations and you'll satisfy your reader. Thus, all great novels have a hero's journey story arc, and all great genre novels follow the rules of genre.

Dare: Does your current Work In Progress follow the rules of story and genre? Discover what they are and work your story into the structure.

Quick Skill: Building a Genre Plot (And why writing in genre makes you a better writer)

I've written forty-five novels. Many of them have been on a best-seller list. A number have won awards. And at least half are...romance.

When I get to that last sentence, whatever literary credibility I've earned with the first three statements seems to vanish. "You write romance?" someone will ask (as if they haven't heard me) and sometimes add an accompanying look of...disdain? Disappointment? As if writing romance is somehow less highbrow than general fiction. I hate the assumption that general fiction is better written. Hogwash.

Words are words, and the truth is, writing fabulous genre fiction is harder than writing general fiction. You have to stand out in the crowd while delivering a plot that follows the genre constructs. General fiction can be wonderful...or it can be a "the emperor has no clothes" moment—everyone thinking the same thing but afraid to say it.

Here's some truth:

~ Genre fiction gives a writer a framework that allows them to hone their craft. Because genre fiction comes with expectations about plot and characterization, the author must adhere to these expectations—and then work twice as hard to make their story unique by using emotional layering and skillful wordsmithing.

~ Genre fiction gives an author a niche in which to sell the novel. It helps them find the right market or line and connects them to the right agents and editors.

~ Genre fiction makes it easier for an author to find a following. If they can construct a story within the structure of genre but with a winning, distinct Voice, fans of the genre will champion them, and their following will build...even if they cross over to other genres. Look at J.D. Robb, aka Nora Roberts.

Here's how to make genre fiction work for you.

Find a genre and stay in it long enough to master it. Work on one element of storycrafting or wordsmithing at a time. In my journey, I used each book as an opportunity to hone dialogue or storyworld or emotional layering or the romantic elements...whatever. Eventually I felt confident in every area, and my books got better with each story.

Study the best-sellers in the genre—what do they do right? Keep a highlighter with you and mark up your stories with passages or techniques that stand out. How can you apply the principles you've learned from these best-sellers to your stories?

Look at the plot constructs—what works, what doesn't? If you're going to have a rogue agent who kidnaps his former handler in a romantic suspense, how does the author make that agent likeable? Or is he? Find the nuances that make a story powerful. Look at the rhythm of when these constructs occur. How do they add to the character's emotional journey and make the story more satisfying?

How can you make your Voice stand out? What unique element do you bring to the genre? I wrote six novels for Steeple Hill/Love Inspired...all of them with an international theme. I lived overseas and could easily write stories set in an international—especially Russian (where I lived)—setting. This became part of my Voice.

Focus on character. Because you are writing inside genre, your plot will be a "repeat" to some extent. So, it has to be your characters who make your stories powerful. Dive deep and create characters who live and breathe.

Genre is an author's friend. Make it work for you as you build your career, and you'll become a better writer.

Quick Skill: Read a genre novel (in your genre!) this week. Write down the genre constructs in the novel and when they occur. How does the author make their Voice or character stand out? Are there any techniques you can apply to your own writing?

Conversation #6: Dark Moment Plotting and how to Build a Story roadmap

"My hero lost his best friend in the war in the bombing of *Pearl Harbor*. He also lost part of his leg."

My aspiring writer, Sally, slapped an open spiral notebook onto the table at the coffee shop and slid into her chair, unwinding her scarf. Outside, the sun shone bright in a cloudless sky, adding a few degrees to an otherwise arctic day.

I picked up her notebook. "I see you've done your homework and discovered a Dark Moment in your character's past and then journaled about it."

"I did that. It was fun—I did the research and saw *Pearl Harbor* through his eyes. In his own words, he told me everything about the attack, and how his buddy died protecting him, and how he wishes he could have died in his friend's place, especially since the guy left behind a fiancee. He made my hero promise he'd look her up when the war was over. I did the same exercise for the heroine."

"This is fabulous." I handed back the notebook. "Last week we talked about the story arc. Today, we're talking about Dark Moment plotting and how it fills in all the big blanks of your Story Roadmap, or story outline. You start by asking your character to tell you about a Dark Moment in his past, or at the beginning of the story, that shaped him, and then ask him to tell it in his own words. By finding that one Dark Moment, you have found all the important elements of his story:

- His Motivation, or what your character wants (which translates into a specific goal, which helps you build the external plot). This becomes his Noble Cause.

- His Greatest Fear, which culminates in the Black Moment Event.

- His internal Lie and his Quest For Truth that comprises the inner journey.

- A potential Wound that has never healed.

She had flipped the page and was making a chart. "Okay, so you're saying that his Greatest Fear is repeating something from his Dark Moment in the past—like, losing his best friend?"

"Yes. You could make him repeat his Dark Moment any number of ways. He could lose someone close to him. Or you could build on his loss. Maybe he falls in love with his dead friend's fiancé, then fears he's betraying their friendship."

"Ooh, I like that."

"The Dark Moment of our character's past will contain many dimensions of fear—we just have to choose the one that works for our story, build it into the plot, and make sure it climaxes in what we call the Black Moment Event."

"I already have the motivation—he wants to pay his friend back for saving his life."

"Which gives you the goal of the story–to keep his promise to his friend to watch over his girl. This is his Noble Cause."

"So, what's the Lie he believes and how does that work?"

"The Lie helps you form the inner journey. Your character starts out believing something that might not be true—like he didn't deserve to live, or he doesn't have the right to love his friend's girl—and through his inner journey, he finds the truth, e.g., yes, he deserves to live, and every day is an opportunity to live well. Or yes, he can fall in love with his friend's girl, and they deserve to be happy."

"So the Lie he believes at the beginning helps us discover the truth he learns in the story?"

"Yes. Your character's inner journey is about going from the Lie to the truth, which is revealed at the Epiphany. There's a step-by-step process of creating the inner journey, but for now, you just need to identify these elements (the Motivation, the Lie, the Fear and the Wound) because you'll use them in your story roadmap, which we'll talk about in a future conversation.

"What about the Wound you mentioned?"

"The Wound is used to heal the emotional brokenness of your character. We're going to talk more about that next week, when I teach you about crafting the Happily Ever After ending. But the Wound is also used in romances. A romance heals the Wound, but the Wound causes the big breakup essential for every romance. So, if you're writing a romance, ask him about his experiences with romance and what he believes about it. Again, have him write it in his own words, and if he has a story to tell, even better. The romantic Dark Moment story might be the same Dark Moment story he told earlier—or a new one. Either works. Regardless of whether you're writing a romance, or not, you need to discover the Wound to help complete his emotional healing in the story."

"Want, Lie, Fear, Wound—got it."

"You'll use these stories in the course of the book for three things:

First: As a way to bond the reader to the characters (and the characters to each other) as they tell their stories, in dialogue.

Second: To deliver backstory in a compelling way, without a narrative dump in the middle of the story."

Third: To craft the essential parts of your plot—the Goal, the

Black Moment, the Breakup (if you're writing a romance), and the Epiphany.

"It sounds…well, not as hard as I thought it might be."

"Getting the Dark Moment story down on paper, in a story, with specifics, is the secret. And look around for the right Dark Moment story. It might not be what you think."

"What's my homework?"

"Once you have the Dark Moment and all the ingredients worked out, I want you to use them to develop a rough story outline for the hero and heroine:

- This is a story about _____.

- What happened to him in the past?

- What does he want?

- How will he attempt to get it?

- What Lie does he believe?

- What bad thing will happen to him?

- What will he learn?

"This will help you understand the flow of your plot. Next week we'll talk about how to craft the perfect, Happily Ever After ending."

Truth: Every story has the same key elements that can be created by exploring one Dark Moment in your character's past.

Dare: Instead of writing a complete bio of your character, try asking him what Dark Moment in his past shaped him (or her), and see if you can make a story outline. You'll be surprised at how well you understand your story in a nutshell!

Quick Skills: An overview of Point of View (POV)

The **Point of View** of your novel is, simply, the person who the story is about, who has taken up the mantle to share the story with the reader. This means the story is being told through the eyes, ears, and mouth of one character at a time. The writer may have multiple characters "telling" the story, but only one is onstage and speaking at the same time.

When you're writing your novel, you'll be focusing on one—or perhaps up to five—characters about whom you are writing. Some of these characters might have smaller POVs (point of views)—meaning they are villains or ancillary characters. As a general rule, however, all major POV characters in a novel should have their own journey—they launch onto a quest, change and grow as characters, experience a Black Moment and Epiphany, have a life change and finish the story with some new—and hopefully satisfactory—situation.

Be a Policeman. Suppose you happen upon the scene of a crime. There is a victim sitting there, as well as his three buddies. You turn to the group and ask, "What happened?" The buddies might contribute to the story in some way, but it is the victim who can tell us the entire tale. Or, if the story is about a buddy who happened upon the victim, you'd tell his story, and the victim would simply be a part of the story.

So, as you look at your cast of suspects, whose story is it? Whose life changes and is affected the most by what just happened? This is your main POV. The others can now step aside and let him/her (or both!) tell the story. But only one at a time.

Let's take a look at this example:

Tom stood to watch the boats docking in the moor. The wind pressed the hem of his shirt against his abdomen as he raised his hand to shield his eyes from the sun. How could he be like one of the boats, free and out on the open sea? His mouth watered at the idea. His heart beat as if he'd actually cut and run.

Behind him, Rachel waited, feeling alone and left out.

Now, what's wrong with this example? I told you what both Tom and Rachel were feeling. That's called "head hopping"—or when something is observed that the POV character can't think or experience.

I read a book review where the reviewer referred to changing POV as head hopping. That's not head hopping. There's a difference between the two.

Changing POV for a new scene is a legitimate and necessary story tool. You change POV by simply inserting a substantial line break, or perhaps asterisks, between the two POVs. Head hopping—telling the reader how two people in the same scene both feel—is not a legitimate story tool. It jerks the reader's emotions back and forth. Who do I feel for in the previous scene? Tom, who wants to be free of his burdens, or Rachel, who feels left out and alone?

Want to convey someone else's thoughts in the scene? One idea would be for the POV character to guess the attitudes or thoughts of the character he's talking to, based on that character's body language, which then would affect the POV character's responses.

Let's rewrite the scene from Tom's POV:

Tom stood to watch the boats docking in the moor. The wind pressed the hem of his shirt against his abdomen as he raised his hand to shield his eyes from the sun. How could he be like one of the boats, free and out on the open sea? His mouth watered at the idea. His heart beat as if he'd actually cut and run.

"Tom, what you are doing? Let's go."

Tom looked back at Rachel. She stood by the car, arms crossed, a frown on her face. She was mad, he guessed, but for the moment, he didn't care.

See the difference? We see the world and Rachel only from Tom's POV. The reader cannot know anything Tom does not. To show conflict with Rachel, I added dialogue. She sounds impatient, doesn't she?

When Tom looks around, we "read" her through his eyes. We get the idea all is not well between them. We are sympathetic toward Tom. Our emotions are with him until, of course, we change to Rachel's POV and we see her side of the story.

When you are composing your story, there are two questions to ask to help determine your POVs and how you will tell your story.

What is your genre?

Determining the POV Voice of your novel starts first with a look at your genre. Romances tend to have two POVs—the hero and heroine. A romantic suspense might have three—the hero, heroine and the villain. A suspense might have two—the hero/heroine and the villain. Women's fiction might have anywhere between one and five. The POVs in general fiction vary, depending on the story, and speculative fiction usually has a large cast.

Once you determine your genre, then ask yourself how many of these POVs will have a complete inner journey? If the story centers on only one or two characters, then it is better to focus on them and simply move the other cast members into secondary roles, without POVs. It can be challenging for a reader to keep track of too many characters, so the rule of thumb is to streamline the POVs—in many cases the fewer the better. When you're trying to get published for the first time, it helps to create a story with the fewest obstacles to publication, and this means adhering to industry standards. You can branch out and experiment after you have a book or two with your name on the cover.

What POV Voice serves the story best?

Voice in fiction has two meanings. "Voice" often refers to how the author tells the story, meaning their style of prose and delivery. John Grisham has a different voice than Stephen King, for example.

POV Voice is used when talking about the verb tense and narration of the story. Stories are most commonly written in third person past tense, third person present tense, first person past tense and/or first person present tense. Occasionally, you might find a story written in 2nd person, but this is rare. Also rare are contemporary stories written in omniscient Voice where the narrator speaks from outside the story.

Let's take a look at the differences between these Voices.

Distant Third Person:

This is the traditional POV, and although fewer books are written in this form, it is still used. Distant third person is often used in the more "narrative" or "telling" forms of storytelling—in the vein of authors such as Nicholas Sparks and Danielle Steele. It's akin to having a character sit down with you and saying, "Let me tell you my story." Then, in third person, they "narrate" the story to you.

This traditional POV is most often in third person, past tense, and will describe situations and emotions as if standing next to, or outside the body of the character. It is also often the Voice of choice in historical fiction. Let's take another look:

When she opened the door, David stood on the stoop, holding the hand of a pretty blonde girl. "Hey, Lisa. I wanted you to meet my new girlfriend, Alena."

Why would I want to meet the girl who has your heart? she thought. "Hello, it's nice to meet you, Alena."

Notice that the thought is in first person and present tense.

Standard Third Person:

This is often the POV used in mainstream romances, although more and more novelists are leaning toward deep third person. Nora Roberts, Debbie Macomber, and other established best-sellers write in this version, which bridges the gap between distant third person and deep POV.

Often, in standard third person, an author will narrate the story as if "telling" the story to the reader....but then dive into first person thought to bring the reader closer. Here it is again with the changes:

When she opened the door, David stood on the stoop, holding the hand of a pretty blonde girl. "Hey, Lisa. I wanted you to meet my new girlfriend, Alena."

Why would i want to meet the girl who had his heart? "Hello, it's nice to meet you, Alena."

Notice that in standard third person, the verb tense stays in past, and the narrative in third person, while the thought is in First Person.

First Person:

This POV is easy to spot—it feels as though the POV character is "speaking" the story. However, true First Person writing is difficult to produce. It is not stream of consciousness writing. In fact, the First Person POV often stands outside the story, then sits down with the reader to "tell" the story, much like the traditional Distant third person. They tell the story from a position of experience or contemplation and are asking the reader to hear their journey:

When I opened the door, David stood on the stoop, holding the hand of a pretty blonde girl. "Hey, Lisa. I wanted you to meet my new girlfriend, Alena."

Why would I want to meet the girl who had his heart? "Hello, it's nice to meet you, Alena."

However, italics are often used when there is a memory voice or another voice screaming in the character's head:

When I opened the door, David stood on the stoop, holding the hand of a pretty blonde girl. "Hey, Lisa. I wanted you to meet my new girlfriend, Alena."

What? No! "Hello, it's nice to meet you, Alena."

If you're struggling to nail the voice of First Person, try writing the scene in Distant third person, as a narration, and then changing it into First. You'll hear the difference.

Third Person, Deep POV:

This is the most common POV in today's contemporary literature. In many ways, Deep POV combines many of the above options, functioning like a combination of Standard Third Person, and First Person POV.

Instead of "telling" the reader the story, Deep POV invites the reader along the journey, unveiling the story through the "first person" experiences of the character. When you're writing in Deep POV anything your character thinks, feels, sees, or hears filters through their head and directly onto the page:

When she opened the door, David stood on the stoop, holding the hand of a pretty blonde girl. "Hey Lisa. I wanted you to meet my new girlfriend, Alena."

Why would she want to meet the girl who had his heart? "Hello, it's nice to meet you, Alena."

It feels like first person, in third person, past tense.

If you're having difficulty choosing which POVs to tell the story in, **ask yourself: who has the most to lose on this journey?** That is the person who will experience the most challenges, and change, and thus, the story should center on them. Likewise, when you're choosing a POV for a particular scene, also ask, "who has the most at stake?" The answer determines the POV for the scene.

Choosing the right POV, POV Voice, and tense for your story is crucial to telling the "right" story. I recently switched a book I'd written three times in first person to third person, past tense—and on the fourth time, created a story worth keeping.

Quick Skills: When crafting a story, consider all your POV and tense options to determine which might be the right fit for the story. Read stories with these various options to determine which one suits your story the best.

Conversation #7: How to find the Happily Ever After ending?

"So, how was your Valentine's Day?" Sally set a red-foil-covered chocolate heart down on the table in front of me and pulled out a chair.

"Lovely. Roses, dinner, and a movie. Sadly, the movie was less than we hoped. I had expected it to be amazing. Gerard Butler, Jennifer Aniston—great combination, right? It had some cute moments, but the fact is, the Happily Ever After—the final kiss—left us wondering if they would survive. Why? Because they never healed the deep Wounds inside them. I wanted to continue our conversation from last week and talk about one more interview you need to have with your character to create the perfect ending."

"Oh good." She set her iPhone on the table. "It's my new recording technique. I'm turning into a journalist with all this interviewing."

"I can admit, I'd love to hear you talking to yourself."

"Some things are private, thank you." She winked.

"A great romance ends with the deep sigh at the kiss of her hero and heroine, right? Well…yes and no. Yes, of course we want the hero and heroine to get together and live Happily Ever After, but if they haven't solved their problems, and their deepest Wounds aren't healed, then it doesn't matter how wonderful the kiss is. After they credits they will return to their darkness."

"I hate that. It's like I know—they won't last, but I can't figure out why."

"Exactly. It's because when we build a story, there are two elements we have to address. The first is the inner truth element. We've talked about this in our last conversation– the Lie they believe and the truth that sets them free. This question is the foundation for the inner journey of the character. But there is more to the character's journey than just the inner one.

"A great romance has an emotional journey, a journey of healing and joy at the end. From the dark places of our past and those things that have hurt us, we've learned a Lie…but we've also received a deep Wound. Something that just…hurts. It could be rejection, or betrayal, or even grief. Often, it has to do with a broken relationship. We carry these Wounds around with us, keeping us away from people who might pour salt into the Wound, or reopen it. Hence why people self-sabotage relationships or veer away from anything substantial—their Wounds simply won't allow them to draw close for the fear of reopening."

"We talked about the Wound last week. Either a part of the Dark Moment story or its own story."

"Exactly. For the romantic Wound, sometime in their past, they've been hurt. If you're not writing a romance, the character will still have Wounds, they're simply not romantic. Knowing the Wound helps you craft the perfect ending."

"What about the Breakup you mentioned?"

"Yes, it helps you craft that, also, but we're going to focus on using it to craft the perfect ending. As we apply it to our HEA ending, we need to start by asking: What is your deep Wound? Why do you hurt? Answering these questions helps you as the author know what you need to heal.

"For example, if we were to use one of my favorite movies, *Return to Me*, the hero states his Wound right out. He will always miss his wife, but he aches for Grace. He aches for that person who fills up his life, completes him. We see this Wound appearing in his Dark Moment, when he arrives home after his first wife's death, takes the dog in his arms, and says, 'She's not coming back. She's gone.' The Wound is visibly played out in subsequent scenes when we see that her absence has wrought destruction on his personal life, turning his apartment to shambles. He is lost without his wife, until he finds Grace. And when she leaves him, reopening the Wound, he voices it."

"The perfect ending heals the Wound," Sally said, leaning over to voice it into her recorder.

"Yes, but that is only one component. Now, you need to give us that moment of delight for not just the character but also the reader. You do this by discovering your character's Greatest Dream.

"The Greatest Dream is something deeper, something sometimes your character won't even know or understand. Let's go back to *Return to Me* as an example.

"The hero's happiest moment is on the dance floor in that happy scene right before his wife is killed. It epitomizes how they belong together. The Greatest Dream for the hero, of course, is to have his wife back. But, we know he'll never have that. The author, however, can delight him and the reader with a piece of his greatest dream and a woman who has the heart of his wife, both literally and figuratively.

"Let's look at the heroine, Gracie. Her happiest moment is getting her heart, but she also realizes that it cost someone dearly. Her greatest dream is to thank the person who gave her the heart and to live a good life, worthy of such a gift. The author delights her, and us, by allowing her to "give" the hero a little something of his wife, yet know that he feels she is worthy of this gift.

"I love this movie, by the way," Sally said.

"Best movie music ever. And the ending is perfect. It's a combination of healing the Wound—for Gracie, being accepted despite the cost, and for the hero, allowing himself to love again—and the

Greatest Dream.

"So how do I find my character's Greatest Dream?"

"Start by asking: What is your character's happiest moment in their past? You want to dig around in his past to find that one moment when everything worked, everything was right. And we want to extrapolate from that some element that we can then use in the ending.

"Again, like the Dark Moment interview, don't let them off the hook by saying: 'When I graduated from college,' or 'When I got married'. Make them be specific. You want to pinpoint an exact event with details. An exact event allows you to take a good look at it, and frankly, if you want, recreate it. Most of all, it allows you to find the minute nuances that pull out exactly why this was the happiest moment."

"Like, maybe it was when she was seven years old, standing in the rain with her father at the carnival," Sally said. "Her hopes for a sunny, bright day are ruined until he takes her hand, and it's that warmth holding her steady that she loves. Her happy moment is knowing she's not alone in the storms of life."

"Interesting, Sally."

She winked.

"Very good. And if your character just can't come up with a happy moment, then try asking: What do you want more than anything and why? Often the *why* will lead to the moment you are looking for."

"I suppose I have to write it down the Dark Moment in detail."

"Yes. This allows you to pull one element of the Happiest Moment story and recreate it or give him that Greatest Dream in some way. Here's the secret: The perfect Happily Ever After ending is one part Wound healing and one part Greatest Dream. You do those two things, and your readers will close the book satisfied."

"Thank you so much. . . now I know what I'm doing this afternoon."

I raised an eyebrow.

"Watching *Return to Me*."

"Don't forget your homework—to wheedle your character into revealing his Happiest Moment."

Truth: Crafting the Perfect Ending isn't about simply ending with a kiss, or saving the world, or catching the bad guys. The Perfect Ending must focus on the character, healing their Wounds and giving them a piece of the dream they never thought they'd have.

Dare: Ask your character—what is your happiest moment? Pull from them a real story, in first person, and you'll find the clues you need to create the Perfect Ending.

Quick Skills: A Blueprint for Character Development and fitting Him/Her into your Story Roadmap

I've heard it said that the harder a book is to write, the easier it is to read. I'm not sure I agree. Yes, a book should cost the author pieces of their heart, but I've found that the more tangled my plot, the more complicated my character, the less popular my stories. As I've grown as an author and learned how to create simple yet powerful storylines and characters, the popularity of my books has grown.

And frankly, as I've streamlined the process of plotting and characterization, the writing process has become easier, also. Sure, it's still hard work and still costs me pieces of my heart as I write emotion onto the page, but I know where I'm going, and the plot is less tangled when I get there.

The fact is, plotting and characterization don't have to be complicated. Your process just has to dig deep for the right pieces.

It needs to start with who your character is…

You accomplish this by digging around for two major backstory elements:

- The Dark moment of his past

- The Happiest Moment of his past, which helps us understand his greatest dream. It can also work with the Dark Moment to help us understand what your character wants.

Here's a quick skills diagram for Character plotting:

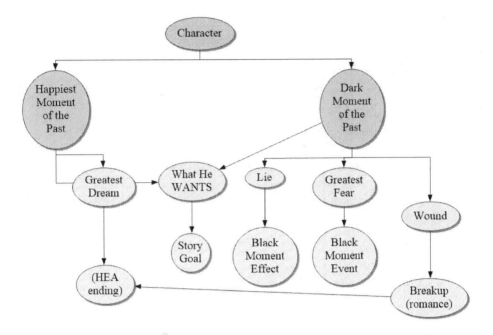

To make sure that I've correctly plotted my character's journey, I ask them, "What can you do at the end that you couldn't do at the beginning?" Donald Maass teaches a variation of this in his *Writing the Breakout Novel*, and I've found it key in my own plotting. This ensures that a character has completed his journey of change…and allows him to win the day, something he can't do at the beginning of the story.

After I find all the pieces, I plug them into my Story Roadmap.

Act 1:

Home World: What my character wants, believes (the Lie), why, and what holds him back from achieving his dreams.

Inciting Incident: The event that propels the character to a possible journey of change.

The Great Debate: The choices before him, and the Push-Pull of the Noble Quest (the motivations that drive him forward).

The Noble Quest: The Quest/Goal that the character will strive to achieve.

Act 2:

The challenges and choices the character makes as determined by his values and his goals, all of which have both consequences and obstacles. This is what I call the Disappointments and Ys in the road.

This Act ends with the Black Moment Event (his Greatest Fear coming true).

Act 3:

Black Moment Effect: (the belief that the Lie is real and that everything is lost)

Epiphany (The Truth that sets the character free—derived from the opposite of the Lie)

Final Battle—Testing of the New Man. That thing a character does at the end of the story that he couldn't at the beginning, to prove that he is changed.

Happily Ever After (The achievement of the dream).

That's it. If it sounds overly simple or structured, remember, it's just a roadmap. You'll discover all the scenes of your story as you build it.

And obviously, Act 2 is much more involved—but I've found that if you get the "bookends" (Act 1 and Act 3) figured out, then finding the pieces of Act 2 are much easier. (Although, I have some Quick Skills hints for Act 2 coming up in a future conversation.)

Hopefully this will help you create a plot free of major tangles.

Now…to the hard work of writing.

Quick Skill: Two powerful interviews, the Dark Moment of the past, and the Happiest Moment of the past can be used to plot your character's journey. Start there to build your plot.

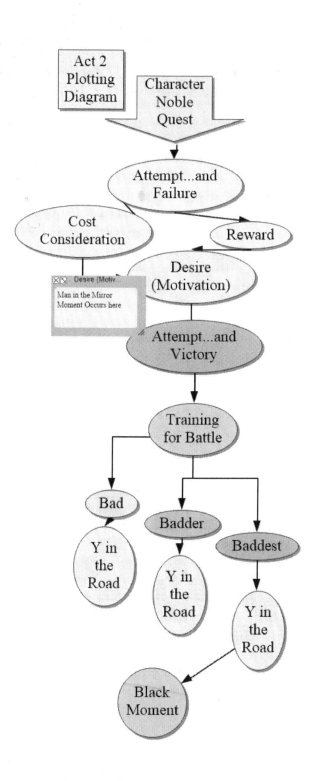

Conversation #8: Plotting the Middle

"I hope you brought your calculator," I said to Sally as I slid into the chair at the coffee shop. Our mid-winter break meant no school, and I noticed her two children playing in the reading nook in the corner.

"I didn't realize I needed to know math to write a novel," she said, but pulled out a notebook. "That may be a deal breaker."

I laughed. "I know I said we'd talk about heroes and heroines this week, but I thought it might be more helpful to first fill in the gaps of Act 2. Last week we talked about plotting, and I taught you how to put together a rough plot. Now you need to look at getting specific with your storyflow, meaning mapping out the pacing of your story.

"This is most easily accomplished by putting together what I call the 'bookends'—Act 1 and Act 3—first. You've already done this by figuring out what your character wants, what his motivation is, and what his home world, Inciting Incident, and quest ate. And, in Act 3, determining the Black Moment Event, the Epiphany, and that thing he can do at the end that he couldn't at the beginning.

"But these two acts comprise only 30-40 percent of your story. For example, for a 90,000-word novel, which is a standard trade-size length, usually Act 1 is the first fifty pages, or about 12–13,000 words. And Act 3 is about the last fifty to seventy-five pages, or about 15,000 words. So, if you do the math, that is about 27–30,000 words, leaving 60,000 for Act 2."

"Why can't I have a longer Act 1 or Act 3?"

"It's all about rhythm. Act 1 is about setting the stage. If you take a long time to set the stage of your story, then readers will complain that it 'took forever to get into the story.' And if you have a long Act 3, then they'll say 'it dragged out the ending.' Keeping both of them succinct solves those problems.

"Here's what I do. I always write twenty-chapter novels. If I'm writing a 100,000-word book, then each chapter is 5,000 words. (I might have two to three scenes within that chapter.) Here's the trick—I always contain Act 1 in the first three chapters. That way, I know I am only using about 15 percent of my novel. If I'm writing a 60,000-word novel, then each chapter is 3,000 words. But I still keep Act 1 within the first three chapters. It's an easy way to make sure I'm keeping the right rhythm."

"That makes sense. But what about the 60 percent in Act 2? What do I do with that?"

"That's what I wanted to focus on today. I call it the 'fun and games' of the story. It's where the challenges, emotional journey, and romance happen. This is also where all the big Turning Points happen in a novel."

"Turning Points?"

"We'll talk about those later—when you have a grasp on the overall plot of your novel. For now, I want to teach you the flow of Act 2. See, as your character starts out on his Quest, after all the Act 1 Home World and Inciting Incident, he is now in the Character Change Journey portion of the story. I've broken it down into four main parts:

The first is Part 1: The Attempt and Failure of the Goal. Now that your hero has launched on his journey, he needs to see what he's in for. If there are no obstacles, if it is too easy, then your character doesn't change and grow, and the story is over. If you want to continue your story, you'll need to give your hero a failure—in fact, make everything worse. This sets him up to really take a look at himself and decide if he wants to go on the journey.

This failure leads to Part 2: Cost Consideration + Rewards.

Right after he or she fails their first attempt, your hero will have to regroup, and take a good look at their weaknesses and vacancies, and realize the truth: If he wants victory, he'll have to change. Another way to put it: Anything worth fighting for is going to cost something.

Give your hero a moment to consider what character change will cost him—and have it be brutal, something that is a true sacrifice. Only then will the sacrifice be truly heart-wrenching.

Now that you've brought your character to their first attempt and failure and given them a glimpse of what it will cost them to succeed, then your character has to see past the Costs to the Rewards. And, they have to believe that it's possible. Or at least that it could be. Seeing the Costs and the Rewards will make them look inside, to ask why that Reward is worth fighting for. (Later, they'll discover what it is inside them that stands in the way.) But for now they have to believe that their attempt and cost is worth the battle.

This is Part 3: The Man in the Mirror Moment (thank you to James Scott Bell for naming this moment for us…it used to be called, simply, Desire. Boring!)

How much is your hero willing to pay for his freedom? To achieve a goal or dream? To save a loved one? To win love? Does the reward justify the cost? In other words, why is it worth it? When you put the cost against the reward, and stir it together, you discover the crux of the heroes' journey…their true desire.

This is where true change begins to take place. It's not about the fears or rewards…it's about the people they want to be. When a character looks inward and asks, "Who am I, and am I willing to change to get what I desire?" then we begin to see true change.

(If you'd like to take a deeper look at this moment, I encourage you to pick up James Scott Bell's ebook, *Write from the Middle*.)

After your hero takes a good look at himself and what he wants, your hero will try again...and this time you'll let him succeed in his quest—just enough to give him a taste of Victory. One game. One touchdown. One completed pass. Enough for our character to feel like they've accomplished something.

The Attempt and Mini-Victory happen in the middle of the Second Act—early enough to leave room for Part 4: Training for Battle.

Your character isn't going to literally "train for battle"—but rather be put through a number of tests. Interpersonal challenges. Physical foibles. Through which, we'll see him have to look inside and make changes.

This is the guts of the book. And the part of the story that is most easily misplotted. For now, follow these principles:

Every obstacle your character faces must make the journey more difficult, causing them to dig deeper and find a character trait that they didn't have before.

They will get "better" at the skills they are developing—whether it be better at completing the tasks the computer tells them to do (*Eagle Eye*), or better at keeping the cell reception and finding the bad guys (*Cellular*), or better at fighting battles (*The Patriot*), or better winning football games, or better at winning the heart of the heroine.

Each time they get better, they become more the person they hope to be, a bigger glimpse of hope... So, give them a glimpse of something they long for. Let them kiss the girl, win the division championship, outwit the bad guys, or figure out why the computer wants to destroy the world.

Sure, your character will have some failures during this section. Some slammed doors, maybe some cuts and bruises, but eventually, they will grow stronger, wiser, more handsome.

Eventually, they're going to feel so empowered that they think they're on top of the world, they've solved the problem, they're on their way to sure victory…

Then you're going to rip the rug from under them and push them right into their Black Moment.

During the Training for Battle stage, I recommend having two to four big events, either physical or emotional, that challenge them.

All of this leads, finally, to the end of Act 2 and the Black Moment Event."

"Okay, I think I understand."

"It'll be easier once you've watched a few movies and seen the flow. For now, here's your homework. Plot the Act 2 Character Change Journey. You're almost ready to write your story summary. By doing this, you'll see the entire journey laid out, and you'll know if your story works."

Her eyes shone. "And then, please, do I get to write?"

"Yes. Soon, I promise."

Truth: Act 2 is the hardest part of your book to plot. The Character Change Journey is a guide to keep you moving forward and give your character the change he needs.

Dare: Plot your character's Act 2 journey.

Quick Skills: Act 2 Character Journey Diagram

I always get the Chapter 7 Blues. I know it's inevitable, but I seem to forget that it happens, and I'll find myself down in the kitchen, moping (and looking for chocolate), and my husband will say, "You're at chapter seven, aren't you?"

I'll turn, stare at him, and nod. "How did you know that?"

"Because the excitement of the story has gotten you through chapter three, and Act 1, and the momentum carried you into chapters four through six, but now the steam has died in the middle of Act 2, and you're down here hunting for inspiration." (This is usually accompanied by him taking the bag of chocolate chips out of my hand.)

He's dead right. I'm smack in the middle of the long highway weaving through Act 2, and it's been a *long* time since I've seen a road sign.

That's when I trudge back to my office and pull out my Story Roadmap. It's not long after that I'm pedal to the metal down the highway, headed to Act 3. All I needed was a little direction. And that's where my Act 2 plotting helps save the day.

To help, I've created a little Plotting Chart for Act 2.

Quick Skill: Plot Act 2 before you start on your journey. You can always change it later as you get into the story, but this way, hopefully you won't find yourself lost in the wasteland of Chapter 7, singing the blues.

Conversation #9: The Black Moment and Epiphany

"Are you ready to finish your book?"

Sally laughed as she sat down at the table in the corner. "I haven't even started it yet!"

"I'm not asking you to write the end of the book, I just wanted to talk to you today about how the Black Moment Event and the ending of your story actually give power to your first act. Think of Act 1 and Act 3 as the 'bookends' of your novel. They are the before and after pictures of your character. Even if they begin in a happy place, there is still something that will cause your hero to become a better person through the book, and they'll end with a lesson learned.

"They learn that lesson by experiencing the Black Moment Event, believing the Lie is real, having their Epiphany, and then changing for what we call the Final Battle. They show they've changed by doing something at the end that they couldn't do at the beginning.

"If you don't know what this Black Moment Event will be, then you don't know what you're aiming for or how to set up the fear that it might happen.

"Let's go back to the conversation we had about Dark Moment plotting. Remember, we examined an event from your character's past and pulled out the Greatest Fear and the Lie he believes. The fear and the Lie are the two things we'll use to craft the Black Moment Event and the Black Moment Effect.

"Crafting the Black Moment Event is all about recreating the Greatest Fear from the past in some way that your character can take another look at it, and this time, find a different answer, one that will change his life for the better.

"Let's say that your character's Greatest Fear is losing someone he cares for. I saw *Frequency* recently, an older movie that I love. The hero lost his father as a child, and he's a mess today, in a broken relationship with his wife, dark, moody, and miserable. Through a miraculous anomaly, he's able to talk to his father in the past through a radio. He warns his father of his upcoming death and saves his life...in the past. Suddenly, the son has all these memories of a wonderful childhood, until he wakes up the next day and finds his mother has died instead. Now, he has to talk to his father in the past to discover why his mother died in the past and stop her death.

"His Greatest Fear happens when both his parents' lives are threatened, and the bad guy arrives in the present to kill him, too.

"The thing is, our hero has never been able to stay committed to someone, to care about them, and the Lie he believes is that he'll never be like his father, the hero. (We see this because he becomes a cop, not a firefighter.)

"When the Black Moment Event happens, the Lie feels true - he can't save anyone (like his father could). The Black Moment Event always causes the Lie to feel true - which is the Black Moment Effect.

"In a convoluted storyline that works—our hero from the present saves his father from the past, who then saves his son from the present. In short, everyone lives. And the son realizes he is a hero. This is his Epiphany. He did change the past - he isn't a failure, but rather a hero like his father. And, in the final scene, we see him with his wife, a son, and celebrating family.

"This is the magic of the Black Moment Event/Effect/Epiphany in a story. It changes your character. With the advent of the Black Moment Effect, your hero learns some truth that he's been blind to up until now. This truth "sets him free" from the Lie, changes him, makes him a new person, and he is then able to do something in the end that he couldn't in the beginning.

"So, before you begin your story, you must know how your character will change. What can he do at the end because of that change? One trick is to show him the opposite way in the beginning. If he will have a good relationship with his daughter at the end, show them at odds in the beginning. If he fears losing his wife to another man, show that fear in the beginning (and make it come true in some way).

"A story is incomplete without a Black Moment Event/Effect/ Epiphany. And, if you don't know where you're going, then it's like setting out to sea without a destination. You don't know how to pack, aside from a swimsuit." I winked.

"So, my assignment is to come up with a Black Moment Event and an Epiphany."

"Yes. Listen, this is fun - you get to see how the story ends."

Sally gathered up her notebook. "I like surprises."

"You can do it, oh Padawan."

Truth: All novels should have a Black Moment Event/Effect/ Epiphany to bring a character to the point of change.

Dare: Craft the Black Moment Event (based on his Greatest Fear), the Black Moment Effect (the Lie feels real) and the Epiphany (the truth that sets him free). What can you character do at the end that he can't at the beginning?

Quick Skills: Black Moment Construction

The Black Moment Event is the most important part of your novel.

I just had to say that, because I see so many manuscripts that pull their punches on the Black Moment. Authors have fallen in love with their characters and they just don't want to hurt them. But creating a powerful Black Moment Event is what both the character and the reader need to convince them they must change.

So, how do you create a powerful Black Moment Event?

First...let's just take a look at the My Book Therapy Black Moment Flow Chart:

As a reminder, we find the Black Moment Event by going into our character's backstory to find a Dark Moment in their past that has shaped them. We ask them to tell us about it (in a journal entry, so we can use it later), and then pull out from it the Greatest Fear and the Lie. The Greatest Fear is the event you will recreate in some form, and the Lie is what you will make your character believe is true and inescapable as an Effect of the Black Moment.

The result of this is the truth setting your character free, to escape thier Flaw, and then a Character Change/Hurrah finale where your character does something at the end that they couldn't do at the beginning.

Now that we have that flow nailed down, let's touch briefly on how to create a powerful Black Moment Event (and Effect!).

- Examine your character's Greatest Fear to find their acute pressure point.

Often, an event like a parent dying isn't the Darkest Moment. It's the moment, two months later, at the father-daughter dance when our heroine doesn't have a date, when his absence sinks in, and the Darkest Moment is experienced. Go to that moment and ask your character: "Why is this your darkest moment?" Maybe it's because he always asked her to dance, and she always turned him down. Or that she spent all year waiting for this dance, and now she has no one to dance with. What does this moment tell her about life, herself, God?

Obviously, when you re-create the Greatest Fear, you can't re-create the actual event. But you can re-create the pain of that event. Regret. Abandonment. Anger? The key is to create a Black Moment Event that produces the same emotions, the same conclusion. The same Lie.

Think outside the box—take it apart, turn it over, and take a good look. It's the not-so obvious moments that are the most profound.

Build that fear in from page one. (This is why you need to know what your Black Moment Event is before you start the novel.) You should slowly be pushing your character to confront this fear (even if they don't know it) with every turn of the page.

You know from the first scene that Frodo fears succumbing to the ring, or worse, having his failure destroy the Shire. You know that Bourne fears he'll never be more than an assassin. You know that Richard Kimball fears letting his wife's killer go free. All these fears are shown in the early acts of the story. Give us a hint of that fear, and the tension will build as we draw near it.

Make the Black Moment Event unexpected yet plausible. Whatever Black Moment Event you choose, it must be something that could happen.

Consider the movie *Indiana Jones and the Kingdom of the Crystal Skull*. Even though critics panned it (too bad—I thought Shia LaBeouf was a great addition), the Black Moment Event works. I didn't like the crystal skulls coming to life to suck out people's brains through their eyeballs and then vanish on a spaceship, but it was classic Indiana Jones. After all, in previous movies, the Ark came alive and punched out people's souls, and then there was the melting man who "chose poorly" in *Indiana Jones and the Last Crusade*. So, even though I didn't like the premise, the screenwriters did build up enough plausibility for it to happen. And, let's admit it—it was sort of unexpected (and creepy!). So, you can get away with crazy, out-of-this-world Black Moment Events if you build up the plausibility.

The Black Moment Event should be strong enough to bring your character to thier knees and re-evaluate everything they believe in. This will lead them to the healing Epiphany. The hero must look back to his mistakes and see what he did wrong. Only then will he come to some truth that will open a new door to a new future. In other words, deal with them on an emotional, spiritual, even values level to make them re-evaluate everything they've believed up to this point.

One of my favorite movies is *Planes, Trains and Automobiles*. I always cry during the Epiphany where Steve Martin realizes that John Candy, his annoying travel partner, has lied to him about his life and has no place to go. All Steve Martin's annoyance is put aside by his gratefulness that he has a family to return home to. His perspective is just in time for the holidays.

Make sure your Black Moment Event rends your character's heart and their Epiphany heals it.

Quick Skill: Construct your Black Moment Event before you write the first word of your WIP so you understand how to increase the tension on every page of your novel.

Conversation #10: The Triumphant Ending

"You might be able to write a book in a month, but I can barely think of a plot! I have four kids, you know." Sally wasn't wearing makeup today, her blonde hair tied back in a ponytail. She looked like she'd lost some weight, her blue eyes a bit tired. "I spent all weekend spring cleaning my house. I haven't touched my story in a week. My ending is so far out of sight, I've forgotten what I'm writing about."

"It's all right, Sally," I said, and nudged my uneaten bran muffin over to her. "You've just forgotten what you're aiming for. See, if you set out on a journey without a destination, you might get discouraged or even…lost."

She tore off a chunk of the muffin. "So, you're saying that crafting the ending of my novel not only helps me with my beginning, but helps me stay motivated?"

"Exactly. Think of your novel like the before and after pictures of a weight-loss journey. The before picture is Act 1, where your character is starting their journey. The after picture is the ending, after the Black Moment Event, Epiphany, and the Triumphant Ending, where they overcome all the things they couldn't at the beginning. The reader needs to see the change, and there is an easy question to help them see it: What can your character do at the end of the book they couldn't do at the beginning? The answer to this is how you construct your Triumphant Ending.

"It works like this: You start your character on a journey, and they have to want something, but be unable to attain it. During the course of the journey, the external plot points affect the internal character journey so that the character begins to want to change, gets tools toward change, and even opportunities to change. When they reach the Black Moment Event, they realize their need to change, and their Epiphany causes this to happen. But in order for us to believe they've changed, they have to be tested. This is called the Final Battle.

"In the Final Battle, they do that thing they couldn't do at the beginning of the book. During the Final Battle, they are again tempted to give up, but they are reminded of the truth (the Epiphany) and finally press on to the Triumphant Ending. This is when we take the 'after' picture. And this is where your reader says, 'Wow, if they can do it, I can too.' Or maybe they simply walk away with some element of truth they ponder.

"In order to build this Triumphant Ending you need a few tools.

"You need to ask: What is the takeaway from this book?

"Another way to put this is to ask: What is the Story Question… and what is the answer?

"From that, ask: How will my character find the answer?

"Finally, ask: What is that thing they can do at the end that they couldn't do at the beginning?

"Armed with these questions, you can build into the beginning of your story the following:

- A glimpse of what your character wants, and why they can't get it.

- A Story Question, subtly woven into the first chapter (and dealt with throughout the book).

- An attempt at the beginning to 'do what they can't do,' and a failure."

Sally had finished off the muffin as we talked. She nodded. "So, you're saying knowing where I'm going will save me from getting lost along the way."

"Yes. It allows you, as the author, to weave in the theme all the way through the story, instead of suddenly inserting it in Act 3. And it allows you to show the complete character change. Finally, it helps you to build a truly triumphant moment into the story by showing that indeed, your character is changed…forever. Love, faith, hope, courage, strength…whatever really will win the day! The truth is, without a Triumphant Ending, the story isn't finished. We just don't know if the character is truly changed. If you want your reader to shout Hurrah! you need to build in the Final Battle and the Triumphant Ending."

"So my homework is to plot the Triumphant Ending?" She wiped the bran crumbs off the table. "And that will keep me moving forward?"

"Yes," I said, smiling into Sally's eyes. "And remember, you will win the day, too. Just keep working. I promise, you will get this story written, one word at a time."

Truth: A novel needs a Triumphant Ending to complete the character's journey.

Dare: Build your Triumphant Ending before you start writing to keep you motivated on your journey.

Quick Skills: The Final Battle Breakdown and Flow Chart

How do you create a Triumphant Ending? We touched on the why in in the conversation, but now we need to put tools to the theory.

Just as a reminder: the point of the Final Battle is to convince the reader (and the character) that true change has taken place by putting your character to the test. Waging an "internal battle," using external elements.

The movie *The Patriot* is a good example of this, because it contains an actual battle, but it also clearly illustrates the internal/external final battle of a story. Armed with the truth, which has caused his Epiphany, the character faces his last challenge, that thing he couldn't do at the beginning of the story that he can now do (or is willing to face) at the end. In this last challenge, he comes face to face with the Lie (or his inner Flaws that have kept him from change). He falters, embraces the Epiphany, and then forges ahead in victory.

If you're familiar with *The Patriot* (and if not, I'd suggest watching it—or at least this part), Benjamin Martin's militia is part of a ruse that entices the British Army into the hands of *the Patriot*s. Everything is going well, but, as the battle ensues, *the Patriot*s falter and begin to retreat. Martin, meanwhile, has in his sights the man who killed both his sons. Martin is running forward to kill him when he realizes that his men are fleeing. So, he has to make a choice—does he pursue his vengeance or help his men stay in the fight?

Martin has always believed that a man can't fight honorably in war. His backstory/Dark Moment is that he committed a terrible crime as a youth fighting in the French and Indian war, and he fears letting rage and revenge master him (something that happened early in the movie and has taken the life of his two sons). He's had his Epiphany—that he can fight for honor—but now, in this moment, he has a choice.

Can he stay the course, fight with honor, or will he give in to a thirst for revenge?

Martin sees his chance, and nearly takes it…until he sees an American flag on the ground. In a very metaphorical moment, Martin throws down his weapon and grabs the flag. Then he turns and calls his men back to action—choosing honor over revenge.

Of course, then, he is free to fight Tavington, having defeated the Lie and realizing he can choose honor over the bloodthirsty man he'd been. Now, let's break that final sequence down:

Step One: Storm the Castle. What is that final thing your character needs to do to prove that they've has changed?

Step Two: Falter, or be attacked by the Lie. How can their fears or Flaws, their Dark Moment from their backstory rise up to make them second guess themselves?

Step Three: Hold onto the Truth! How can they be reminded of the truth or Epiphany?

Step Four: Seize the Day—Victory! How do they complete their journey by showing they have confronted the Lie, and chosen truth? How can they win?

I like to define the steps that I've just outlined and let the story and characterization take it from there.

One of the tricks that really helps me is to post the sequence of the Final Battle on my computer as I write so I know where I'm going. It keeps me motivated that yes…there is a Triumphant Ending!

Quick Skill: Creating a Triumphant Ending is all about staging a Final Battle. Create the steps and you'll ensure a powerful character change ending for your story.

Final Battle Visual

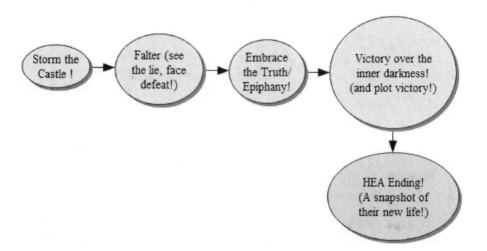

Conversation #11: 3-ACT overview

"I think I just need to sum up." Sally sat on the deck of the coffee shop, staring out at the lake, the waves frothy along the shore as it coughed up the debris of winter. A spring fragrance seasoned the air, and from the earth around the deck, irises braved the crisp Minnesota air. Any warmer, and we might be out here in our shirtsleeves, so anxious we are for summer.

I sat down, lifted my face to the sun. "Sum away."

"I just want to make sure I have the three acts correct. I know we discussed them all, but I just need to make sure I understand the overall flow of story structure."

"I'm all ears."

"Okay, in Act 1, our character walks onto the page fully formed, with a Dark Moment in his past that has created a Greatest Fear, a Wound, and a lie. He has a greatest dream, based on something happy in his past he wishes he could attain, but something is holding him back from this. He also has something he wants, expressed in a goal. This is called Home World, and where I start the story—"

"Unless you start with the Inciting Incident," I said. "And then insert Home World next."

"Right. The Inciting Incident is the unexpected event in his world that causes him to have to make a decision and go on the figurative journey that is the point of the rest of the book. The result of the Inciting Incident is something called the Great Debate, where he has to look at all the reasons why he should go on the journey versus the ones holding him back, and then he makes a decision to move forward into the journey, often called the Noble Quest.

"This is the end of Act 1 and the beginning of Act 2. Act 1 comprises the first 15 percent of my novel."

"Yes." I leaned down, rolled up the cuffs of my jeans. My ankles, at least, would get tan.

"Act 2 is what you call the Fun and Games. It's where my hero grows emotionally and discovers the Lies and hears the truth that leads up to the Epiphany. But not before he has his Black Moment Event. Act 2 is comprised of the character launching out on his Noble Quest and failing. Then he has to decide whether it's worth it and then goes forward into a series of tests that will equip him to try again for what he wants. During this time, he will have triumphs, disappointments, and conflict to push the story forward, all of which enhances the Black Moment Event that is looming at the end of Act 2. Act 2 cumulates in the Black Moment Event, which is his Greatest Fear coming true."

I rolled up my shirtsleeves, glanced over at her, and nodded.

"Act 3 begins with the Black Moment Effect, which is part of the inner journey, and is the Lie feeling true. The hero feels a death of his dreams, yet in this moment, he has his Epiphany as the truth hits him and he is set free. He is now able to do something that he couldn't do at the beginning of the book. This is often called the Final Battle—the proof of the character change. The hero is tested as he faces his biggest challenge but finds victory in the end by clinging to the truth. Act 3 ends with a glimpse of the new Home world, and the Happily Ever After Ending. Act 3 is about 15-20 percent of the novel."

I grinned at her, warm all the way through. "Well done. Now, your homework is to put those pieces together into a story summary. Just lay out the big pieces. As you do this, you'll be able to see if you have your pacing correct and if you have all the elements you need for the overall structure of your novel. And, if you haven't done this yet, you'll need to create a Story Map for every POV character who has a journey in your story."

She leaned back and lifted her face to the heat of the day. "Sure is beautiful today, isn't it?"

"Indeed," I said. "But don't get too comfortable. You still have more work to do before you can start fleshing out the story."

She waved me away. "Just let me enjoy the day."

Truth: Figuring out the three acts of your novel helps you see it in a nutshell and helps you understand if you have a compelling story. It gives you confidence that you can write a great story.

Dare: Do you have all three acts outlined for your novel? If not, build the key ingredients before you start your synopsis, or even your writing. Even if you change the plot or the scenes as you write, you can still stay on track with the big picture.

Quick Skills: Lindy Hop Diagram

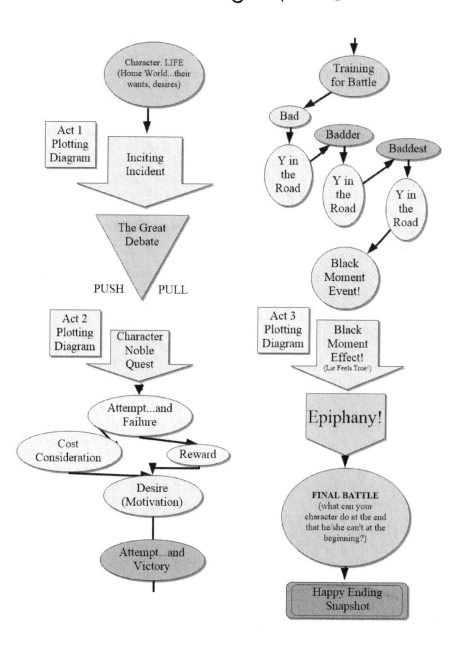

Act 1 Plotting Diagram

LIFE (Home World...their wants, desires)

Inciting Incident

The Great Debate

PUSH

PULL

Noble Quest

Act 2 Plotting Diagram

(Noble Quest)

Attempt...and Failure

Cost Consideration

Desire (Motivation)

Reward (taste of what they will get if they continue)

(Disappointments & Ys in the Road)

Training for Battle

(1) Bad

Y in the Road

(2) Badder

Y in the Road

(3) Baddest

Y in the Road

Attempt...and Victory (This can occur any time during the

Training phase)

(HELP!)

Black Moment Event!

Act 3 Plotting Diagram

Black Moment Effect! (Lie Feels True!)

(OVERHAUL)

Epiphany!

FINAL BATTLE

(What can your character do at the end that he/she couldn't do at the beginning?)

Perfect/Triumphant Ending

Conversation #12: Tips for Unravelling the Plot into a Story

"I'm stuck." Sally said as I hung my purse on the chair and shucked off my jacket. Outside, the last remnants of a late-season snowfall clung to the ground. I'd had to dig out my Uggs again for a trip to town for our weekly chat.

"Good," I said.

"What do you mean, good? I thought you were rooting for me!"

"I am. But let me guess—you've put together all the big pieces, but the middle looks like a black hole, and you're afraid it won't come together."

She narrowed her eyes at me. "How do you know that?"

"I've written forty-five books. I know what happens in the middle of the weeds of plotting." I smiled at her and sipped my coffee. A raspberry white-chocolate indulgence.

"I did everything you told me to do—plotted the Black Moment Event, figured out the grand ending, even came up with the Act 2 fun and game events that cause him to grow. And still I'm stuck."

I nodded. Blew on my coffee. "But have you told yourself the story yet?"

She frowned at me. "I know the story. I dreamed it up."

"Maybe. But the fact is, until you sit down and tell it to yourself, you can't see the Flawed motivations, the dangling story threads, the implausible plot nuances, or even the magnificent metaphors and themes. You have to tell the story—preferably out loud—to spot these things. So, when I hit the wall after my speedy first act beginning, the sure cure is to sit down and tell myself the story. Which means…write the synopsis."

"I feared you were going to use that word today."

I laughed. "Think of a synopsis as the story, in a nutshell. The only reason it feels overwhelming is because you're worried about other people reading it. For now, let's say it's just for you, so it can be as messy and tangled as you want. You'll straighten it out, clean it up, and make it sparkle later. For now, your synopsis will serve as your roadmap to get you from chapter 7 to the end."

"I have to tell myself the entire story? It just sounds exhausting."

"You're about to write an entire book. I'm asking you to invest four hours in the summary to see if it will work. Would you rather wait until you've invested six months to discover you've hit a wall or are writing in circles?"

"But doesn't that take the fun out of the discovery of the story?"

"Listen, if you're going to Boston, does it take the fun out of the discovery of Boston if you plan your trip a little bit? No. It just helps you know how to pack and know what sites you shouldn't miss. That's what a story summary does—it points you in the right direction. The discovery happens when you get into the scene. And again, you can change the story at any point, if you'd like, but at least for now, you have words on the page.

"But here's the good news…you'll know if your story works. And that's essential, because frankly, that's what's holding you up right now…the fear that your story won't work, right?"

She made a face. "I guess I need to tell myself the story."

"Your homework for the week. Keep it three to five pages, single spaced. I promise, you'll be glad you did."

Truth: Telling yourself the story in synopsis/summary form helps you discover story holes and motivation Flaws, and keeps you from wasting words and time.

Dare: Can you tell yourself the story?

Quick Skills: How to get your Story Summary onto the Page

I know that people panic about writing a synopsis. The fact is, there are many different synopsis styles and deliveries. There is no one right way—but there are a few principles.

Let's start with Delivery:

You can write the synopsis a couple different ways. First, you can tell the story as if you were the narrator:

This story is about Maggie, a former Red Cross nurse who lives in World War II New York City. More than anything she wants to get over the grief of losing her fiancé during the attack on *Pearl Harbor*, but her life seemed to stop the day she got the news, and she doesn't know how to start it again. Until, one day, she runs—literally—into a man named Peter. Peter is a sailor who received a medical discharge after nearly losing his leg during the *Pearl Harbor* attack. He is bitter and angry—not at his injuries, but at the fact that he let his best mate die. More than anything, he'd like to go back and save his friend. But there is no way to atone for his mistakes.

Except, there is. Because Peter's friend was Maggie's fiancé, and there might be a miracle at work that night when they meet....

You're simply telling the story from a bird's-eye view.

The second way to tell the story is a "Police Report." Think of the POV players as the eyewitnesses to the story, and you have to file a report as to what happened. You'll start with bios of the witnesses, and then let them each have their turn telling the story, each interjecting their motivations and decisions for their actions as the story progresses.

Let's pick up our story and continue it with this method. Although it ends up sounding similar on the page, sometimes it's easier to get the story points onto the page.

Peter can't believe that a beautiful woman has nearly plowed him over on New Year's Eve—and he's even more horrified when she sees his injury. Probably he shouldn't have been so rude to her—especially when he spies her later, crying. What's a guy to do? He reintroduces himself and discovers that she's crying over a lost love. He understands that kind of grief, and in an effort to comfort her, invites her to Times Square to celebrate the New Year.

Maggie calls herself a little crazy when she agrees to leave the New Year's Eve party with a virtual stranger. But somehow Peter doesn't feel like a stranger. There's something about him she finds familiar, and it's this feeling that woos her into a cab to Times Square. Maybe it's a sign that yes, she can start over....

With this method, you are going back and forth in POV, still keeping it third person, but letting each player tell "their side of the story."

Regardless of which method you use, you must always consider this: For every action, there is a reaction, which leads to a new action. We'll develop this more when we talk about scene construction, but for now, always ask: Is there a good reason (motivation) why my character reacts this way? A good reason (motivation) for his decision as he proceeds to the next action? Whether or not you have solid motivation for your characters' actions will become evident as you tell yourself the story.

Now, let's talk about tone.

You can write your story in third person, past tense, third person present tense, or even first person (although this is rarely done, I've seen it done successfully). Regardless, the key is to write your summary from a bird's-eye view—you're taking a pass over the story, resisting the urge to "land" and explore key moments. Don't skim over everything and then slow it down and tell us how the hero caresses the heroine's face before he kisses her and declares his love.

Just say, "Jeremy declares his love." Then keep flying. The synopsis is not a place to showcase your elegant wordsmithing (although yes, you want to make it interesting).

A word about wordsmithing…

After you have the synopsis written and you're ready to submit, now it's time to smooth it out. Go through and add in "color" words—powerful nouns and verbs that add an emotional element to your story. Use active verbs instead of the passive. Tighten sentences. Search for overwriting, and delete.

If you need to, refer back to your Story Roadmap Chart.

Most of all, don't panic. Get yourself a cup of coffee and settle down to hear a great story…yours.

Quick Skill: Sketch out the three-act structure, then tell yourself the story, making sure you have a motivation for every action your character takes (and every lesson they learn). You'll use your Synopsis to help you write your novel.

Conversation #13: Discover your Hero and Heroine

"Today, you officially write," I said to Sally as she plunked down her bag. She appeared frazzled, her blonde hair pulled back into a frizzy ponytail, and she wasn't wearing makeup.

"Good, because I need some writing therapy," she said as she sat down. "After a week with the kids home from school for spring break, it's time to escape. In fact, I might have already started." She handed me four pages of her manuscript. "It's the first scene."

I scanned it. "No, it's not," I said. "It's a smattering of the first scene and a lot of backstory." I handed it back to her. "But it's a great start. And you've done what I would have suggested you do—sit down and start writing that first scene. I expected you to do just this—start telling the story, and then load in a lot of backstory and narrative about your hero."

"But isn't that information important? Like knowing where he went to college and his job and why he went into the military and how he wants to be a doctor but he can't afford the training so he's a medic?"

"Yes, it's important…later in the story. And that's what we're going to talk about today—delivering your hero or heroine to the page in a way that makes them seem alive and three-dimensional. Your goal here is to let your character walk onto the page fully formed, thinking and acting as if you suddenly dropped in on him in the middle of his day.

"Consider this. I saw you walk in today, and even though I didn't know what your life was like this week, your demeanor and appearance told me you'd had a rough week. If I were writing this, in your POV, I might have said this:

"She just wanted one hour without the kids hanging on her. Sally slid into the chair at the coffee table and managed to untangle her bag from her shoulder, realizing she still had enough kid supplies in it to last her and her brood for a week should they suddenly be stranded by the side of the road. Real business-like. She'd have to figure out how to balance her four kids, a tired husband, and her decade-long hope of being published. She took out her notebook, pushing away the thought of the mounds of laundry at home. This hour belonged to her."

I got a glimmer of a smile. "That sounds about right."

"Now, if you were a reader, you'd know a few things about Sally. She is married, her kids demand a lot from her, and she has some conflicting values between writing and mothering. We also know that she is pursuing a lifelong dream. We don't really need to know any more than that. And I told it all through her eyes as she walked in. I can teach you some storyworld techniques later to layer in her emotion, but for now, think of it like this:

"As you walk into the scene, you're in your character's head. Everything your characters sees, thinks, and feels filters through her point of view, or POV. Your job as the author is simply to be that character. Don't tell us what the character is thinking, just think it. Don't tell us what they feel, just react to it. Open your mouth and speak, and let the character come alive.

"Think about it; do you know someone from their bio, or from experiencing the journey with them? This is what you're offering your reader as you open your story—a taste of the journey, and an invitation to come along.

"You'll give them a hint at what is at stake, and the kind of person they'll spend time with, and even the goal and main problem you want to solve, but that's all. Don't bog us down with a bio about your character and who he is—which is what you wrote in this first scene. Get us into the story.

"Here's a tip—if you feel you have to write the bio for the sake of understanding the character, that's fine. Just start the story in chapter two, then file chapter one in the 'for the author only' file. Your story starts when your character stops explaining who he is and what he's done to this point and gets up and begins to engage in the journey."

She nodded. "I think I get it."

"Now here's a few things you need to get across in the first chapter. First, we need to know who your character is—and what I mean by that is, what his personality is, what he believes about himself, and life, and what he wants. You do this through his mannerisms, what he says, what he thinks, and how he treats the situation he is in. This is 'showing,' and is the best way to get the story across. Oh, and don't make him perfect—remember, he has to have a Flaw and a fear if he is going to be real. By the way—you need to do the same thing with the heroine."

She was looking at her manuscript, circling things, crossing out others. "I think I understand. It's like I'm just starting the story on this day of his life, cutting into the action, not introducing him like he was speaking at a seminar and then opening the story."

"Yes. Remember, you've already done the hard work of character creation—figuring out his identity, his Wound, his Happiest Moment, and all the added character elements about him. Now, you just need to let him walk onto the page. Next week, we'll talk about the two different kinds of romance structure. Now…your homework is…go write."

Truth: Your character needs to walk onto the page without any backstory baggage to get the story going quickly, and you do this best by getting in the skin of your character.

Dare: Try writing the scene without any backstory at all. Read it over—insert only the information you need to justify your character's actions.

Quick Skill: Creating Heroes and Heroines—Tips and Tricks

How do you make your hero or heroine unique? Have you ever created a hero or heroine and thought…oh, they seem just like the last character I created? It's easy to do—you can only pick so many creative combinations for your character… *unless…*

…Unless you go about character creation from the inside out. I've talked about finding an identity for your character unique to him and building the "outside" to match that inside identity. However, I have a quick trick to help make him even more unique. To make him stand out on the page without going over the top.

We're going to start with identity again, but this time we're going to focus in on your character's Greatest Fear. We've asked him about his Dark Moment of the past and discovered that fear, and now we're going to build a Flaw out of that fear.

Consider this: A man's Greatest Fear stems from the Dark Moment in his past when his father's drunk driving accident killed a man in their small town. Our hero has always walked around with this stigma and fears one day doing something to brand his own family. His fear is disgrace. So, his Flaw stems from that—he is overly conscious of "doing the right thing." So much so, it actually immobilizes him, because he fears saying the wrong thing. He is often tongue-tied, maybe even wishy-washy, maybe he runs himself ragged trying to be all things to all people. His Flaw is that he never really gets angry (even when he should), because he fears it.

Now, let's take it one step further. I am going to create one mannerism that shows this character Flaw. Maybe he presses his hand to his chest, taking a deep breath when he is confronted with a problem. Maybe he stutters. Maybe he gets migraines, so he is always rubbing his temples. Maybe he drinks milk whenever he goes into a bar. The key is, I'm trying to connect his behavior with his Flaw.

Now, I'll use this mannerism in the story in a couple of ways.

First, I'll have the character simply behave this way as a part of his character makeup. I won't explain it away with some sort of back-story narrative I'll simply embed it into his characterization.

And, somewhere in the book, I might have someone mention it. "I think you need something stronger than milk, Jerry," the bartender says to him when he sits and simply stares at the milk on the bar as his life falls apart. Or he's in his office with his head in his hands, rubbing his temples, and his secretary brings him a glass of milk and aspirin. "You're allowed to get angry, Jerry. Preferably before your head explodes."

Whatever the mannerism may be, now you've made it a believable element to your hero, based on his unique fears and Flaws.

Quick Skill: Find your character's fear and ask: What Flaw results from this fear? How can I manifest this Flaw in a mannerism or behavior? (Or even a physical attribute?)

Conversation #14: The Basics of Writing a Romance

Sally came into the coffee shop with a smile. "My husband gave me the entire weekend to write. I've written five chapters since last Monday."

"That's a good man you have there," I said. "And a good model of a romantic hero. This week, we're going to talk about how to craft your romance."

"Oh, I know how to do that. I'll just make them fall in love."

"That's, of course, the goal, yes. But along the way, we have to doubt that they will, indeed, live Happily Ever After. We do that by creating obstacles, or what I call, Why Nots—both internal and external—that feel so big that they can't overcome them.

"Consider this—if you know how much a couple has overcome to be together, isn't it more moving? We want to root for them. But if there is no reason to believe they won't make it, then why care? Without obstacles, there is no story, and especially no romance."

"I guess that's why making up after a fight feels so good."

"Yes. And that's exactly what you're giving the reader—that sense that love won the day. To do this, you need to find both an internal and an external obstacle that keeps your hero and heroine apart. The external obstacle can be derived from the plot, something that is obvious. Classic examples are: He owns the bank that is taking over her land. She was in love with his brother. He is her boss, or took her job. She bore his child and didn't tell him. Of course, you need to get more creative than that, but those are examples."

"Like, my hero failed to save the life of the heroine's fiancé?"

"Yes. And you can add to that the loyalty he has to his friend—he'd never marry the man's fiancé. Can you say *Pearl Harbor*?"

She smiled, gave a shrug. "But it works, right?"

"Yes. Then you need to look inside for the internal obstacle. His guilt keeps them apart. And she fears loving again after being hurt so terribly. You look at their internal Wounds and use those to keep them apart."

"So, if their obstacles are so great, how do they overcome them?"

"Why does anyone come together? Because the reasons to be together outweigh the obstacles keeping them apart. You build in what I call Whys, or reasons why they love each other. The reasons are based on three elements—shared values, the fact they make each other better people, and the sense that they complete each other. Look for these elements, and build romantic scenes that emphasize these Whys as you build your story. You'll use the Whys after you create the breakup moment in the story—near the end—to help them remember the big picture. But the key is—make sure your Why Nots are at least big enough to overcome the Whys at the moment they need to breakup. It's only after they breakup that they'll realize they can't live without each other…and you can write the Happily Ever After ending.

"And before you ask, yes, they have to breakup. Because, again, we need to believe that true love will keep them together, and it's only when it's tested with the breakup—and then the sweet reconciliation—that we believe they will last.

"Your homework this week: find the Internal and External Why Nots, and the three Whys for your hero and heroine. Then, plot some scenes that will reveal both of these."

"I just want to get to the kissing scene," Sally said as she gathered up her notebook.

"Don't we all."

Truth: All romances must have Why Nots as well as Whys to craft a romance a reader will root for.

Dare: Ask your characters why they can't be together, internally and externally. Then ask them what they love about each other. Then, insert the answers into your story (in dialogue). It'll build the believability of your romance arc.

Quick Skills: Finding your Romance Story Arcs

If you are writing a romance, it can sometimes be difficult to know exactly how to fit all the pieces so that you have the right amount of tension in your story. How soon do you make your characters fall in love? When do you start breaking them up? How do they get back together?

This problem is solved by understanding the two main story arcs of romance: The Why/Why Not and the Why Not/Why.

Understanding the kind of story you have helps you understand how to layer in the tension and where to insert the different components of your romance.

Let's a take a look.

The first structure is Why/Why Not:

These are stories that have our characters falling in love in the beginning, with no major obstacles in their way, only to discover obstacles halfway through the story, or even later. It's not about how we as the reader see their journey, but how the characters see it. We know what they don't.

Return to Me: The hero and heroine meet and instantly hit it off. They have a similar sense of humor, and they like similar foods and have fun together, even have some romantic sparks. Until she discovers she received his deceased wife's heart when she got a heart transplant. Suddenly we've arrived at the Why Not part of the story.

You've Got Mail: The hero and heroine love each other online, have similar interests, similar love of New York and books and business drive. They are perfect for each other until they find out they are enemies in real life. Enter, the Why Not.

The key to the tension in these story arcs is that the reader knows why they will breakup, even if the character doesn't. It's waiting for that breakup that puts us on the edge of the seat/page.

Let's look at the other structure: the Why Not/Why stories.

In a Why Not/Why story structure, the external and internal obstacles (Why Nots) keep the characters apart even as the Whys pull them together. Then, when it seems that the Why will win the day, the biggest Why Not rises to break them apart.

Sleepless in Seattle: The hero and heroine have so much Why Not in front of them, it seems they'll never get to the Why. Again, it's in the viewpoint of the character, not the reader, because from the beginning we can see that these two belong together. Why Not: She's engaged to someone else, they live thousands of miles apart, she doesn't even know him, he thinks she's loony (or at least among the strange women writing to him). It's not until the end that they realize they belong together and discover the Why.

While You Were Sleeping: The Why Nots are glaring. He's her, um, fiancé's brother. And of course, she lies to everyone, but that only adds to the Why Not, until she's revealed as a liar. But by then, they've seen the Whys, and that is what causes the angst.

As you're beginning to plot your romance—even before you nail down the component elements—think through the structure of your story. Do you have the Why first and then the big Why Not? Or is the Why Not glaring, until finally the Why is too big to ignore?

In the early stages of my plotting, I start with creating the hero and heroine. Then I assemble a few of the key ingredients: why they belong together, why not, what their sparks are, their happily ever after. Nothing is written in stone, however.

Then, to get going, I nail down the story arc: Why/Why Not or Why Not/Why. Knowing what kind of story arc I'll have helps me know where to drop in the components. For example, if I'm building a Why/Why Not story, I'll build the interest, throw in some wooing and Why elements, as well as the kiss, and perhaps even a glimpse of the happily ever after at the beginning. (They need to know what they have to live for!) Then, I'll throw in the Why Not, with lots of sparks, and the Black Moment Event.

If I have a Why Not Structure, then I'll start with sparks, a touch of interest, perhaps a hint of wooing, all the while keeping the Why Nots paramount, gradually leading up to the kiss, before we get to the big sacrifice and the Why.

Quick Skills: Is your romance a Why/Why Not or a Why Not/Why?

Quick Skill: Figure out your Romance structure and it will help you build the right kind of tension in your story.

Conversation #15: Should I write a Suspense?

"I think, I want to write a suspense thread into my romance." Sally sat down at the coffee table. Outside, the sun shone, spring was in the air. "I watched *Eagle Eye* on FX over the weekend, and I realized how much I love suspense."

"I love suspense too," I said. "A romantic suspense combines the fun of falling in love with that edge-of-your-seat fear that the people we care about could get killed.

"Let's take a look at what that would mean for your story. Writing a romantic suspense means adding another story structure/plot to your novel. You'll have to learn to weave the romantic beats in with the big suspense elements in the right rhythm. The good news is that you can often combine some of the big moments of romance and suspense so they merge. For example, the heroine or hero might meet at the onset of the suspense. And the final battle/grand gesture or sacrifice can be combined in the final sequence. But I'm getting ahead of myself. Let's talk about the structure of a suspense.

"First, know the difference between a mystery, a suspense, and a thriller. A mystery has a dead body at the beginning. The suspense has the dead bodies along the way. And the thriller has the threat of dead bodies at the end. Of course, there are often dead bodies throughout all of these, but the threat is emphasized at different points in the plot. *Eagle Eye* is part thriller because the big event is at the end, and part suspense because we are driven through the story in one suspenseful scene after another. To figure out the genre, and the structure, you have to identify the 'Big Event' in the story.

"For example, *War of the Worlds*, an alien invasion movie with Tom Cruise, has the Big Event happen at the end of the first act, and yet the terror continues as the aliens chase after and eliminate the Americans. The story is a suspense."

"The Big Event in *Eagle Eye* is the assassination of the president," Sally said.

"Good. It's a thriller. Every event leads us to something bigger—heading toward the big finale. Once you figure out what that big finale is, you must set up the suspense along the way."

"How do I do that?"

"Early in the First Act, you have to set up the hero and heroine as the likely players in the suspense plot—and you have to give them a good reason for being there. For example, in *Eagle Eye*, the hero and heroine are picked in what seems like a random act, but they are also the only ones who figure out what is going on and can stop it.

"Then, you have to set up a villain, and/or an antagonist who is causing the threat, or keeping them from saving the day. And you'll have to give him a reason for being there, as well as work him into the plot.

"You'll also have to plot external conflict related to the suspense that will keep them away from their goal. Some of the conflict in *Eagle Eye* results from the hero and heroine's mutual distrust of each other and the impossible odds of them accomplishing their tasks. Then they must together face a computer/villain that controls everything.

"Finally, you'll have to give them the ability and motivation in every scene to overcome the obstacles and save the day. One trick I've discovered in writing romantic suspense is that the suspense thread winds up before the romance thread."

"Do I need to plot the suspense thread separately?" Sally made a face as she looked up from her notes.

"It helps initially to plot it separately, just to make sure you have all the key plot points for your suspense. But then you can weave the plot into the emotional and romantic journey. One thing to remember is that the word count for your novel doesn't increase with the addition of the suspense thread—you have to write tighter to get it all in. But romantic suspense continues to be a strong seller in the market, so it's something to consider."

Sally took a deep breath. "Maybe I should just finish the romance, and then think about the suspense."

"Or, write this one, and we'll work on a romantic suspense next. It might help to get one technique mastered at a time."

"So the truth is, I'm not quite ready for a romantic suspense?" She gave me a wry grin.

"I'm not saying that. I am saying it might take starting over with a new plot, or at least extensive rewriting. It's up to you, but writing a romantic suspense isn't about just inserting a guy with a gun—it takes an overhaul of the plot."

She tapped her pen on her paper, looked outside at the thaw, back at me with a smile. "So what's my homework?"

"Take the week and read a suspense and find all the big pieces. This should help you decide whether you're ready to tackle this thread."

"I think I already know the answer."

Truth: A romantic suspense novel has equal parts romance plot and suspense plot intertwined. Both must be fully fleshed out and then combined to create the right balance.

Dare: Read a romantic suspense novel and see if you can find the big event, the motivations, and special abilities of the hero, the heroine, and the villain. Identify where the suspense and romance threads intersect.

Quick Skills: The Key to Suspense: The Big Event

We love the end of basketball season every year. Why? Because the final NBA games bring us one sport closer to football. We love football, and the wait between January and August feels interminable. One of the things I love about football is that it's a great metaphor for nearly everything.

Like writing a suspense novel. A football game has all the elements of a great suspense novel: If the team doesn't have the ability to lose, (or win), then we won't believe they can lose, (or win). We also need to care about the team, so they have to be heroes under all that gear. The game only lasts for four short quarters, so there is an immediacy to the threat (and a deadline). And finally, there must be a villainous team opposing them that makes us believe that all could be lost.

We're going to touch on the one big element every suspense should have: the Big Event.

Every suspense must have a Big Event that looms in front of the character. It's an Event they must either stop or achieve in order to save the day. The story may begin with a sample Big Event and lead up to another one. Or, it might have the Big Event in the middle, with the aftermath climax at the end. But the reader must believe that something terrible will happen if the hero/heroine doesn't succeed, otherwise, there is nothing "suspenseful" to worry about. The key is that while the story builds up to that event and the closer we get to it, the more obstacles are thrown before the hero/heroine.

Let's take a closer look at the Big Event. Whether the event that will happen is caused by a natural elements or a villain, it needs to have four components:

The Event must be Believable. You can accomplish this by showing a similar or like event happening in the beginning of the book or a small glimpse of what could happen if things go awry. If I were writing a football book, I might have my undefeated team lose a game by a lot, to show that our team could go down, hard.

The Big Event also needs to be Compelling. If it doesn't affect the life of a character that we love, then we won't really care. Or, if it doesn't affect them in a way that matters to us, we also don't care. It has to be personal. This is why high school football is way more exciting than professional football. It's my boys out there on the field, fighting for our small town.

There also needs to be an immediacy or a Deadline to the Event. Four quarters, that's it. The hero/heroine/readers must believe that the threat/Big Event will happen, and soon.

Lastly, we need to believe that this horrible Big Event will be... Horrible. Terrifying. Awful. This is different from believing it can happen. It's answering the question — so what? If it happens, how does it affect me?

For homecoming one year, our high school played a team we hadn't defeated in six years. They liked to rub our defeat in our faces. To make us bleed, hurt, and hang our heads. Not this year. We held them to four overtime goal line stands and beat them by a touch-down.

It was the most terrifying three hours of football I'd ever experienced.

Believable, Compelling, Immediate, Terrifying—the four components of the Big Event.

Quick Skill: If you're writing a suspense, think of it as a sporting event (preferably football) and build in the components of the Big Event.

Conversation #16: Writing the First Chapter

"I'm angry with you!" Sally said as she sat down. She was smiling, so I wasn't worried. "You let me write the first chapter before I was ready."

"Oh, that," I said. "Yes, I did. But I knew you had so much story in you that if you didn't get started you'd only get frustrated. I know why you weren't ready, but you tell me."

"I didn't really know what my character wanted, or how to hint at his Greatest Fear in the first chapter, so I created exactly the wrong scene."

"You created the scene that helped you jumpstart your story. You were doing a lot of "Wax On, Wax Off" and getting ansty. So, I told you to simply let your character walk onto the page and let him start talking. Did I know you'd have to rewrite your chapter? Yes. But every author has to rewrite—it's a part of the process. I encouraged you to write for three reasons:

"First—it gave you a chance to hear your character speak and see if he fit the profile you created for him.

"Second—it allowed you into the story, to get excited about writing and see your words on the page. Part of writing is just the success of building scenes and chapters and then believing you can do it all the way to the end.

"Third—It made my job of convincing you that you needed to start in a new place easier, because you saw the story, but realized that it needed to move faster." I smiled. "Authors often think we have to lay out all the information about a character in the beginning. I wanted you to get that out of your system so you could go back and rebuild the chapter with just the essentials."

She made a face at me, then smiled. "Okay, Mr. Miyagi, what are the essentials of the first chapter?"

"I watched *Frequency*, an old, but favorite movie this weekend. I love the opening, because it so well captures all the elements of the first chapter/scene. The story is about a fireman and his son, and how they reconnect via a time/sunspot anomaly. It's a thriller, fabulously plotted, and if you have a chance to see it, you should.

"The first two scenes of the movie capture what I consider the five essentials of the first chapter of a novel.

"They set up the character's Competence (or what he does well).

"They set up his inner journey issue—the father is too much of a risk taker (the bicycle scene).

"They set up the hero's Greatest Fear—that he'll take too much of a risk.

"They show what both characters want in a very poignant moment when another character, the 'Little Chief,' sees what they want, or what their focus is—a great family.

"They contain something that ignites the plot, or the Inciting Incident. In this case, it's the aurora borealis. Remember, because this movie is a thriller, these first scenes also set up the suspense plot.

"All of these elements are wrapped up in the hero's home world—the five Ws—who he is, when it is, where it takes place, what he does for a living, and why (his current motivations).

"By the end of the first chapter, your reader has to know through the action and dialogue these five things: Competence, Lie, Ignition/Inciting Incident, Fear, Focus/Want. I made it into a nice little acronym for you, because that helps me remember it. Think of it like a CLIFF…and you are about to send your character off it. You want us to see him before he goes flying into the story."

"So I'll bet my homework is to rewrite the first scene so that it shows these five things."

"Exactly. Here's the truth. A great novel isn't written—it's rewritten. (I don't know where that quote comes from, but it's not mine.) Sometimes you just need to let your character speak to you before you can craft that first scene. But if you want to build a solid story foundation, you have to start with him on the edge of the CLIFF."

Sally was somewhere else. Then she looked at me and smiled. "I'm not angry at you anymore," she said.

"I'm very glad to hear that."

Truth: The first chapter is the most difficult. While you might hurry into a story because you want to get it onto the page, you'll most likely need to go back and rework the first chapter with all the elements. Remember, your first chapter is also the most important chapter of your book.

Dare: When you're ready, go back to the beginning and craft the first chapter with the five essentials.

Quick Skills: Five Essentials of a First Chapter

There are a lot of checklists for building a first chapter, and sometimes they can get overwhelming. So, let's start building that chapter one with five essential elements. This is actually step two in your process of writing that first chapter. As Sally and I talked about in our conversation, sometimes it just helps the writing process to let your characters walk on the page and wander around a bit. We can hear them, talk to them, discover if we have profiled them correctly. No, these wanderings probably won't be the final first chapter, but it gives you a chance to get some words on the page.

But after that initial jump into the story, you need to go back and craft a foundational first chapter.

Let's start with five elements. You're starting your story at the edge of a CLIFF:

Competence: Show that your character is good at something and can eventually win the day with these skills.

Lie: Where your character will start their inner journey.

Ignition: Set up the Inciting Incident. Perhaps it's just the hint of the Inciting Incident. Maybe it is the actual event. But hint that something could be happening…even if you are setting up a perfect world situation, we will then suspect your character is about to fall hard.

Fear: We want to know what your character fears—maybe he sees something, says something. It's usually very subtle, but it's something that we can look at later and say, yes, we saw what he didn't want to have happen!

Focus: We want to see what your character wants, what his goals are. What is he about?

Because you know your character, you should be able to craft this scene. If not, start with a character interview.

Questions to ask your character to help build the first chapter:

Competence: What are you good at? What are your super power skills that we can highlight now to show how you'll save the day at the end?

Lie: What Lie do you believe and how do you show this in your everyday life?

Ignition: What will happen in this chapter, big or small, that will change the life of your character and ignite him on his journey?

Fear: What fear hangs over the charater and how can you hint at it in this first chapter?

Focus/Want: How can you express your character's focus in this chapter? Show who they are and what they want.

The final step is to wrap all of this up in Home World, inserting the five Ws—Who, What, Where, When, and Why. These should give you the framework of your first chapter.

Here's a hint. Don't write, just talk through the scene with a friend or craft partner. Confirm that you have captured all the elements. If you haven't, rewrite the scene. Now that you know what you're looking for, you can build the scene verbally before you get it on the page (but remember to take notes of your conversation!).

Remember, you don't have to get the scene right on the first pass… you're still in rough-draft mode. Just shoot for these five basic elements. You will go back later and add in the advanced list (coming soon!) to bring your scene to publication level.

Quick Skill: Start the first scene with your character on the edge of the CLIFF…ready to take off into the story. Build the five elements—Competence, Lie, Ignition, Fear, Focus—into your Home World, and you'll have a powerful foundation for your story.

Conversation #17: Crafting the first Sentence HOOK

"I'm sorry Sally, I don't have much time today. I'm on my way to the airport." I unWound the scarf from my neck and slid into the chair. "But I did want to talk to you quickly about Hooks and First Lines."

I pulled out the printed e-mail she'd sent me. "I have your new draft here. You did such a great job of pulling me into the story and deleting all but the essential backstory. Now I want you to take a look at that first sentence.

"Most authors don't start their stories out in the right place, and even when they do, they struggle to nail that first line. I often write the first line last, after the book is written, because by then I know what the book is about—the theme, the tone, the most compelling element, and I put that into the first line. Consider your first line as a promise of everything you're going to fulfill in the story.

"There are four different ways to start a story. I made a list, with examples from literature:

"A Voice. I don't love starting with Dialogue, because we don't know who is talking, but sometimes it can be effective in first person. For example,

"'Call me Ishmael.' (*Moby Dick*)

"Or maybe something from contemporary literature:

"'If you really want to hear about it, the first thing you'll probably want to know is where I was born, and what my lousy childhood was like, and how my parents were occupied and all before they had me, and all that David Copperfield kind of crap, but I don't feel like going into if, if you want to know the truth.' (*The Catcher in the Rye*, J.D. Salinger)

"This works because we are immediately introduced to the character and get into their head. Ultimately, we are wooed by their personality.

"Persona. Start your story with the description of someone iconic. Someone that stands out in our minds.

"'There once was a boy name Eustace Clarence Scrubb, and he almost deserved it.' (*The Voyage of the Dawn Treader*, C. S. Lewis.)

"Or, 'Scarlett O'Hara was not beautiful, but men seldom realized it when caught by her charm as the Tarleton twins were.' (*Gone with the Wind*, Margaret Mitchell)

"Note that both these Voices are omniscient, but you could build a strong character introduction through the Voice of a POV character.

"Consider the opening to John Irving's, *A Prayer for Owen Meany*. 'I am doomed to remember a boy with a wrecked Voice—not because of his Voice, or because he was the smallest person I ever knew, or even because he was the instrument of my mother's death, but because he is the reason I believe in God.'

"If the character will have a profound impact on your story or your POV character, perhaps start with a snapshot of that character.

"Reminiscing. Many coming of age stories start with a step into the past, some statement that sums up where the character finds themselves today.

"I did this in *Everything's Coming up Josey*. I started with the line,

CONVERSATIONS WITH A WRITING COACH

'It's important to acknowledge that Chase was right and if it weren't for him I might have never found my answers.'

"Basically, it's a summary of the past, spoken from the present. And the rest of the book is about proving or revealing the impact of this reminiscence.

"Here's one from the *Great Gatsby*, F. Scott Fitzgerald. 'In my younger and my more vulnerable years my father gave me some advice that I've been turning over in my mind ever since.'

"Statement. I like to start stories with a strong statement. A statement of opinion or fear or hope.

"Jane Austen does this in Pride and Prejudice, 'It is a truth universally acknowledged that a single man in possession of a good fortune must be in want of a wife.'

"When you make a statement, you are setting up the Story Question in a novel. You'll spend the rest of the book making a comment about or proving your statement.

"Your Character's first thought. This is a technique I use to get the reader right into the POV of the character. It is not internal monologue, but rather a thought captured in that moment that encapsulates the stakes, the emotions, the fears and the problem of the book. I always put it in third person, so it's very similar in feel to the statement, above, when delivered in third Person Deep POV.

"This is from my book, *Take a Chance on Me*. 'Ivy Madison would do just about anything to stay in the secluded, beautiful, innocent town of Deep Haven. Even if she had to buy a man.'

"I'll teach you this HOOK method in the upcoming Quick Skills."

Sally took the page from me and read her first line aloud. "Walker set down his coffee and dug into his eggs. How he missed his mother's cooking." She looked up. "This is right before he hears the explosions as the Japanese bomb Pearl Harbor. It starts right at the beginning of the action."

LearnHowtoWriteaNovel.com 121

"I know. And it's not a bad place to start. But what if it started with the bombs already dropping, or perhaps, with him trying to save lives? And what if what is at stake is whether he will live, or whether he can save the man next to him? Then, how might you start your first line? Perhaps with a snapshot of the person he will save? After all, the entire story is about Walker spending his life trying to replace him."

"I hadn't thought about that. I just wanted to get right into the story."

"You could also start with a statement about the war, perhaps, something deep in Walker's POV. That would get us into his character and give us something that he might wrestle with the rest of the book.

"We spend so much of our time wanting to get right into the scene, we don't stop to think about the profound impact the first line has. You want to move into action, but first, delight your reader with something that will make them think, something that whets their curiosity for the rest of the story. The truth is, a reader does want to get into the story, but they also want to be charmed by the first line. That's your job as the wordsmith." I took the pages back. "I need reading material for the plane. But your homework is to come up with a killer first line for next week."

Truth: Woo your reader with your wordsmithing from the very first line of your novel.

Dare: After you've written the first chapter, go back and rework your first sentence. Have you raised the curiosity of your reader? Are you wooing them into the story?

Quick Skills: Hook Your Reader on the First Page.

I love this quote by Gabriel Garcia Marquez, who won the 1982 Nobel Prize for Literature for *One Hundred Years of Solitude*:

"One of the most difficult things is the first paragraph…in the first paragraph, you solve most of the problems with your book. The theme is defined, the style, the tone. At least in my case, the paragraph is a kind of sample of what the rest of the book is going to be."

By the way, that book sold over 10 million copies. The hook paragraph, your first paragraph, just might be the most important paragraph you write in your entire story. I'm going to share with you my technique on how I figure out the first sentence.

I use an acronym, SHARP, which stands for:

Stakes

Hero/Heroine identification

Anchoring

on the Run

Problem (Story Question)

Before I write anything, I start with understanding the big picture of my story and my scene.

Step One: Figure out what is at Stake.

Stakes drive your reader through the story, and hinting at them in the beginning will give your reader "something to fight for."

Public Stakes: Public stakes have much to do with public values, what matters to people. Ask yourself: What matters to me? If it matters to you, then it matters to others. What's the worst thing you could think of happening to you? Others fear that also. And that's where you find your Public Stakes.

Personal Stakes: Personal Stakes are used in conjunction with Public Stakes to bring the danger/dilemma/fear home to your POV character in a way that personally touches him. A great example of this is *24*—even when Jack is trying to save the world, he is also concerned about saving someone he loves. *Pearl Harbor* matters not only because of the attack, but because of the tribe of people we've come to care about in the story and the lingering fear that Danny and Rafe will die before reconciling their friendship. Even *Independence Day* uses this technique to great effect: Will our heroes return (after blowing up the mother ship) to the women they love?

Private Stakes: Private Stakes can be found in the roots of our values. The things that drive us, or the things we long for. Private Stakes work when the main character must choose between two equally important values to succeed. *Saving Private Ryan* is a great example of a movie that embodies Private Stakes. Should you sacrifice many to save one? Or how about *Sommersby*? Should you die for a crime you didn't commit to save the woman and family you love?

How do you find those personal values of your character?

To find the Private Stakes, ask:

- What matters most to him in life?

- What would he avoid at all costs and why?

- What defining incident in his past has molded him to the person he is today?

- What are his goals and why?

Take two of his values, and then ask yourself: In what situation would these values be pitted against each other? These are the Personal Stakes.

Beyond the Public, Personal, and Private stakes of a story, you'll also have stakes for every scene. These stakes are found by asking: What could go wrong in this scene? This question will create the backbone of tension in your scene—and something you should consider when crafting the first line.

Step Two: Create Hero/Heroine Identification, or Sympathy for the character from the reader.

You're trying to create a connection with the reader by helping them identify with the character, making them feel their pain, fear, and even joy. As you start your story (and every subsequent scene) you want your reader to feel sympathy for your character. How do you find that sympathetic element?

Ask yourself: What do I have in common with my character? What need, dream, situation, fear, or past experience do we share? And what about that can I use in my story?

Step Three: Anchoring, or using the five Ws to create a sense of place.

By the end of the first paragraph, and for sure the first scene, you should have anchored your character into the scene by using the five Ws. Who, What, Where, When, and Why? The five Ws can evoke emotions and give us a feeling of happiness, tension, or even doom in the scene.

Ask: What is the one emotion you'd like to establish in this first sentence, paragraph, scene? Using the five Ws, what words can you find for each W that conveys this sense of emotion? You'll use these in the crafting of your first paragraph.

Step Four: Start your scene on the Run.

Dwight V. Swain says in *Techniques of the Selling Writer*, "A good story begins in the middle, retrieves the past, and continues to the end." Your first sentence hook should be something that begins in the middle of the action, with the story already in motion. I like to think of it as the moment you throw back the curtain in a play—movement is already happening.

- Step Five: Set up the Problem or Story Question.

  As we've already discussed, the Story Question is the one thematic question that drives the book. This question permeates all the decisions of the hero and/or heroine throughout the story and needs to be hinted at in the sentence in the first paragraph, and in the first scene.

- Just as a review, remember to ask: What is the lesson my character will walk away with? The question that accompanies that answer is the theme.

- You could take these five elements and sift them together. Or you could highlight one of these elements to serve as the first line.

- Or, try this—if you are writing in Deep POV, ask: What is my character thinking right now? Could this thought serve as the first line?

- Quick Skills: Know all the key elements of your first scene before you begin writing the first line. Then you can make it compelling and raise the reader's curiosity.

Conversation #18: The Basics of Scene Rhythm

The sun tugged at the irises peeking from the dirt edging the coffee shop. Another month in the northland, and spring might actually arrive, cascade into summer. I found Sally at our table, grinning at me.

"What?"

"Now that I know my characters and my story structure, I think we're coming to the best part—the scenes."

"You're right. At least, that's my favorite part about writing. Because we can talk big picture and characters all day long, but when you create scenes, you are bringing the story to life. Think of every book as a collection of scenes, or live action that we can observe, like a movie. In fact, for me, writing is not unlike viewing a movie…I close my eyes, see the scene, and walk through it with the reader."

"That's what I see too. A movie in my head."

"And people laugh when we say we hear Voices. They're real people talking to us." I winked at her, and she laughed.

"There is a rhythm to storytelling with scenes, however, that is important to learn that will help you craft a book with the right motivation and pacing. And that rhythm is achieved by the right combination of Action and Reaction Scenes.

"An Action Scene is one with activity, a scene where something happens. A Reaction Scene is just that—the reaction to what just happened. I often use the example of the shootout at the OK Corral. The shootout is the action—the reaction is the part where they hide behind the haystack, reload, and figure out what to do next. Then, after they figure it out, they jump out and start another action scene.

• "An Action Scene has three parts—a goal, a conflict, and a disaster. For every Action Scene, the POV character will have a goal (as will the other characters). It must be specific and clearly definable, and it must be a proactive goal, something that makes our character alive and interesting.

"However, standing in front of that goal are obstacles your POV character faces on the way to reaching his goal, which causes conflict. You must have conflict in order to make the scene interesting, and ultimately to help your character grow.

"Your Action Scene must end with a new problem that contributes to the overall Black Moment event, and causes your character to have to make a decision about their next course of action. We've talked about these Ys in the road before."

Sally nodded, her gaze past me, as if she might be thinking. "So, falling in love with the hero in the beginning of the book might be a disaster, because we know he has a secret that will break her heart."

"Exactly. Which bring us to the Reaction Scene, or the emotional and physical follow-through to the disaster. A Reaction Scene has three parts also—a response, a dilemma, and a decision. •

"Your POV character and the other characters affected by the disaster are reeling and will need to process and hurt and panic and be afraid. This scene gives your reader a chance to react to the situation along with your character.

"Then, your character must take stock of his situation, look at his options, worry, and think through the what-ifs. This is the dilemma. Eventually, the character will come up with a decision.

"Once he makes a decision about what he will do next, your character establishes a new goal—one based on his values and his motivations, and most of all, his Noble Quest. A Reaction Scene ensures that you have the right motivation for every proactive decision and action your character makes.

"Now, you're back to a scene. This is the rhythm of a well-knit story, and is a powerful tool in creating a page turner. Think about your book as a collection of scenes, and you will be able to draw your reader into the moment and create a book that will imprint on their mind."

"So, is my homework that I go through my first scenes and make sure they are Action or Reaction scenes?"

"Yes. Up until now, you've been writing by instinct. But if you want to make sure your pacing is right, you need to build the right rhythm into the story.

"As you start writing your scene, begin with the question: Is this an Action or Reaction scene? Once you know this, you'll know what components to build into the scene. In later weeks, we'll add to these components to help you build tension in either kind of scene."

Sally closed her notebook. "I'm a knitter. And when I start a project, all I need to know is how to knit or purl. Then I start looking at the blueprint and begin to knit. Pretty soon, I've knit an entire slipper. I feel like I've finally figured out how I might write this story all the way to the end."

Truth: The rhythm of Action and Reaction scenes ensures that you have the right motivation for every proactive decision and action your character makes, and keeps your story moving along at a consistent pace.

Dare: Can you identify the Action and Reaction scenes of your novel? Do they have the three components necessary in each scene? If your story lacks the right pace, or your characters lack the right motivation for their actions, try doing a realignment.

Quick Skills: Scene Development Tips and Tricks

There are three stages to the discovery stage of writing a novel: Character development, Story development, and Scene development. Like building a house, the book takes shape as you craft each scene.

In the previous conversation, we went over scene rhythm, how an author knits the story together through Action and Reaction scenes, and the components of each. Here are some tips as you work through each component.

Action Scene Tips:

Goal—A character has an overall story goal, but inside those goals are smaller goals, goals derived by the situation or his motivation or the events happening around him. For each scene, make your goal specific, tangible, measurable, and timely. This will give an urgency to your scene and will make your character alive and interesting. A character who wants something desperately is an interesting character—someone we want to know or emulate. And this helps a reader bond with the character.

Conflict—A scene without conflict is a *boring* scene. The conflict can be internal, competing values or external—something physical that stands in the way of the goal. There are two tips to creating great conflict:

Make it visible to the reader—we need to believe that the conflict is real, not imagined.

Make it equal in degree to the character's motivation for completing the goal. Conflict that is too easily overcome isn't a real conflict. That's why bad guys are stronger than good guys—because if they weren't, there wouldn't be a story. That's why there is *always* kryptonite in a Superman story. So make your conflict strong enough to defeat your hero.

Disaster—Another way to explain this is that there must be something new at stake at the end of a scene, something that raises a new risk, something that adds an element of looming disaster. The disaster must be something that contributes to the overall Black Moment Event of the story. A disaster might actually be a victory or the character reaching their goal at the end of the scene. For example, I might give my character a job opportunity, with the caveat that if she doesn't do this well, she'll lose everything—which of course, she then does! As you plot the disaster that looms at the end of your scene, ask: How will this scene ending make the Black Moment Event blacker?

Your disaster must also be compelling enough to make the reader turn the page. If there is no sense of dread or disaster, no sense of anticipation, then the reader won't continue.

Ask: Does my disaster make my reader care more about the character, enough to turn the page?

The disaster can be found by asking the following questions:

What is the worst thing externally (circumstance or physically?) that could happen to my character?

What is my character's worst fear at the moment?

What is the worst information my character can receive right now?

What is the worst trouble my character can get into in this scene? Raise the stakes so that they are further from their overall goals.

Have I set up the danger for the readers before the scene begins?

Have I made my reader *care* about my character? Can they sympathize? Spell out the stakes often enough so the reader worries!

Now, let's take a look at the Reaction Scene Tips:

Response—The importance of the Reaction scene is to understand what just happened and ti give your character the proper motivation to continue his journey. This starts with a response to what just happened to the POV character in the scene. Go back to the last scene he/she was in—even if your character was not the POV for that scene. How does he/she feel about what happened? Give them an emotional response to it so the reader can catch up and see how the character affected. Then, they have to consider their options…or the dilemma before them.

Dilemma—The next step in a Reaction scene is to have your character see his choices before him. When an author leaves out a perfectly reasonable option and takes one that feels contrived, it cheats the reader. The key to building a great dilemma is to make sure your character sees all the options before him and takes them all into account as he considers what to do. Then, give him good reasons for dismissing them.

Decision—Your character will finally make a decision, based on his values and his motivations. Here's the key: It's important that your character make the decision for himself, not have the events just push him along. But make the decision something that makes sense to the reader, one they can get behind. If you have to make a decision that isn't popular, make sure you rule out the obvious decision with a good reason.

A fast-paced story will have Reaction scenes cut down to the bone. A longer story will draw them out. And, you may even combine a Reaction Scene with an Action Scene to keep a story moving faster in Act 2, or near the end. But you must have a Reaction Scene, however long, to build the right motivation into your Action scenes.

Now you're ready to move into the next scene, an Action Scene.

Quick Skill: The Action/Reaction scene rhythm will help you build the right motivation for your character all the way through your story.

Conversation #19: What is Scene Tension?

"Happy Mother's Day, Sally," I said, while holding a plate of basil mashed potatoes and beef medallions. I couldn't wait to get my hands on that broccoli salad—the house specialty–and eyed it as another patron of the Sunday Brunch dived in.

Sally looked up as she spooned smoked salmon onto her plate. "Hello." She glanced behind me, and I saw one of her children, the six-year-old, heading for the buffet line.

"How's the writing going?"

"Good," she said as she reached around me, handing him a plate. "Don't spill." She stepped out of line. "I don't know if we can meet tomorrow. I have a school field trip."

"No problem," I said. "We were just going to talk about Scene Structure."

She made a face. "Okay, I lied. The writing is not going well. My scenes just feel so...boring. I keep trying to add some action, even obstacles into the scene, but it just ends up looking like a lot of activity—James, that's enough olives!" She made an apologetic face as she turned back to me. "Sorry. He's like a football player–could eat you out of house and home."

I laughed. "I had a couple of those. But I know what your scene is missing—tension. It's that sense that something could go wrong, that the character isn't going to meet their goal." Another patron bellied up to the broccoli dish. Shoot. Maybe I could elbow my way in, take out that woman and her walker.

Sally, meanwhile, edged toward the buffet table, reached in, and righted her son's plate before his gravy could hit the floor. "But I can only put up so many obstacles before the scene seems silly."

"Obstacles aren't tension. Tension comes from the inside, from fearing something will—or won't–happen, or even wanting two different things. For example, right now you fear James will dump his mashed potatoes and gravy on the person in front of him."

"You don't know James. Last month, he managed to spill Kool-Aid across three plates at the church social."

"I understand. You want to allow him independence, and for him to succeed at getting his own plate of food, and yet you also don't want to make a scene. Those two goals, together with the obstacles that your son is young and you're trapped talking to me, is causing you great tension."

She gave me a wry smile.

"Creating more obstacles doesn't create more tension. Tension is created in three ways:

"By fearing something and trying to keep it from happening.

"Needing something to happen and fearing that it won't.

"From wanting two equally valuable things, thus creating inner dissonance.

"In your case, both of those things are happening right now, and you're just about to grab your son's plate and tell him to go to the table, which could possibly create a huge scene, which is a fear, also."

"You're a mom, aren't you?"

"Of three big sons who had their share of buffet moments. But every scene has tension embedded in it. You just have to figure out the fear that looms over the scene."

Oh good, the servers were adding more broccoli. I turned my back on it to focus on Sally.

"You do this by figuring out what your character wants, and why, and then using your obstacles to keep your character from achieving it. Or, if they eventually do achieve it, by making us believe they won't achieve it until the very end."

She smiled as her son walked past her, a slab of roast beef draping over his plate. He made it all the way to their table. "So tension in a scene doesn't have to be bombs blowing up, or people getting shot."

"No. It can be simply a mom trying to keep her son's Sunday shirt clean in the buffet line. The key is, it has to be something that matters to the character, something they want, for a good reason. The obstacles simply threaten that thing they want. And it's this fear of failure that creates the tension. You can also increase the tension by having your character want two different things, and have an inner battle about which one is better."

"Like standing in line talking to my mentor, or helping my son navigate the buffet line."

"Right." I smiled.

"So, instead of meeting tomorrow, how about if I figure out what my character wants and why, and what might stand in her way."

"Great! That's your homework this week. And in Quick Skills, I'll share with you the equation I use for creating tension in a scene." I headed back into line to grab the broccoli spoon. "Happy Mother's Day."

Truth: Obstacles in a story are not Tension. Obstacles in a story create tension by standing in the way of what the character wants. To create strong tension, start with what the character wants, and why, and then add the obstacles. This combination will create a fear of failure. And that fear is what causes Tension.

Dare: Do you have a fear of failure in your scene? How about using two different things your character wants to create inner tension? If your story lacks this, go back and ask, "What does my character want, and why?"

Quick Skills: Scene Tension Equation

I just finished Book 2 of *The Hunger Games* series, *Catching Fire*.

Excuse me while I go pick up Book 3 and spend the day ignoring my to-do list. This series is a lesson in how to create fabulous tension. Not only is the story premise fraught with tension, but every chapter has that "can't put down" quality.

Why? Tension on every page (as the master Donald Maass would say!)

But what is tension? Recently, I read approximately 1,768,639 contest entries. Okay, not quite that many, but it felt like it. And very few wove real tension into their story. Obstacles and Activity are not Tension. Tension is a combination of a Sympathetic Character + Stakes + Goals + Obstacles + Fear of Failure. If any of these are missing, we don't have tension.

But how do you build that tension into a scene? Here are the questions I ask that help me craft scene tension:

What does my POV character want? What does he/she want at this moment? Emotionally, physically? What makes him/her relatable and sympathetic? Once I ask this, I have to ask: Why? Why do they want this right now?

To answer that question, I employ something I call the Push/Pull. The Push/Pull helps build the motivation to move your character into action. Every scene has to have an emotional or physical Push/Pull (or combination thereof). It's the Push away from something negative, and the Pull toward something positive.

So, for example, your hero wants to stay at home and protect his children from the aliens. But he knows that his children are a distraction, and last time the aliens attacked, his son tried to help and nearly got them killed. (The negative Push). He also knows that he can probably defeat them if he joins with the other fathers on the block (Positive Pull). So, he decides to leave his children behind and attack the monsters, a decision that goes against his instincts but makes sense once the Push/Pull is added.

But I'm not finished. To add tension, I need to ask, what will happen if they *don't* meet their goal? What fear hovers over the scene? These are the stakes of the scene. Without stakes, without something that could go wrong and they could lose, there is nothing to fear.

All of this boils down, then, to your character's Goal. This is something specific, measurable, achievable, realistic and timely and must be driven by the Want and the Why. Without a goal, you can not create scene tension because you must have something driving your character forward, to push against the obstacles.

What are the Obstacles?

What will stand in the way of your character achieving this goal? Obstacles can be people, situations (weather, machines, or even government), or a person's own emotions/values. They must be big enough to challenge the character's goal, but not so overwhelming he won't even try to defeat it. A great obstacle brings out a new character trait in your hero that helps him rise to the occasion and drives him further along the character journey.

However, the key to tension is the reasonable Fear of Failure. A Fear of Failure is found by looking to the end of the scene and asking: Will your character reach thier goal?

If not, then hint that they will in the scene, make them believe they'll have victory, only to disappoint them at the end.

If yes, then hint that they will fail, only to surprise them at the end.

For example, in our earlier scenario, ask: Will our hero defeat the aliens? If yes, then have him face seeming failure at least twice in the scene—maybe once when all the men fall and he is injured, and then again when the aliens find his hiding children (only to have his son emerge the victor!).

Or, if our hero does not defeat the alien, give him a taste of victory in the scene so we believe he will, first with the heroes finding the aliens and taking out their ship, and then with them defeating the alien captain—only to have the entire alien army show up and chase them back to their homes.

We'll revisit this concept later, during editing, but building these elements as you write your rough draft helps you build tension with every scene.

Quick Skill: Do you have all the components of a Tension-filled scene? Check the equation! (Sympathetic Character + Stakes + Goals + Obstacles + Fear of Failure)

Conversation #20: Keeping Scene Momentum going between Chapters

I feel like it's been forever since we've last talked," Sally said as she came into the coffee shop. "And with Memorial Day today, and the fact I haven't written recently, I feel like I've lost all momentum on my chapters."

Outside, Kathy was planting geraniums in the coffee shop planters. The sun glinted off the lake, and the fragrance of lilacs hung in the air. I had a tan from the weekend and couldn't wait to get home to our family barbeque.

"Oh, I hear that," I said. "I haven't written for five days. It can be frustrating when you walk away from your novel with your ideas still trapped in your brain. One of my biggest frustrations in writing a novel is that I can't write it all in one sitting. Seriously. I've tried. I once wrote a novel in ten days. It's a good thing my people brought me food! I love being able to write a novel in a concentrated amount of time, because the storyline is never far from me, and while it's exhausting, the story always seems to emerge with fewer jolts in the plot. But life doesn't work that way, does it?"

She shook her head.

"So yes, let's talk about how to keep momentum going between chapters even when you have breaks in writing. The first thing you need to do is to interview your POV character about the previous scene they were in.

Ask the following questions:

1. What did you think about what just happened?

2. What are your choices?

3. What will you do next, and why?

4. What is the worst thing that could happen to you right now?

5. And, if it's a romance –how do you feel about this person? What do you fear happening emotionally?

"It helps me get into thier head and start mulling over the next scene as I go about driving my kids to football practice, or getting on an airplane to speak at an event.

"The interview also helps me put together the pieces of the next chapter and establish the next step by asking: What are my Action Objectives?

"The Action Objectives are the things that help me understand what I as the author have to accomplish. It's all the movement, information, inner and outer journey steps, and any hints of future trouble I need to insert.

"Once I understand these, then I go through the scene setup, deciding the Action/Reaction elements, Setting up the SHARP elements (Stakes, Heroine ID, Anchoring, Run, Problem (or Story Question), and then begin with the five Ws to set up the foundation of the scene.

"I know it can be difficult to get back in the groove of a chapter after walking away, but you can do a tremendous amount of prework on your scene by simply asking—and answering—the right questions while you are doing laundry, shopping, driving, homeschooling, and even exercising. Then, when you're ready to write, you'll have all the pieces you need."

Sally was busy scribbling. Quiet.

A long time.

"What are you doing?"

She looked up. "I'm doing my homework–interviewing my character."

Of course. "I'll just leave you two here for some privacy."

Truth: Momentum in a story is about picking up the threads from the previous scene and continuing them into the next scene.

Dare: Interview your characters after/before every scene to keep your story fluid and moving forward.

5

Conversation #21: Keeping your Reader Hooked through every chapter.

Sally came into the coffee house dressed in a pair of jeans, an old sweatshirt, and a baseball cap. "Don't laugh. I told my husband I'd go fishing with him today. He has the day off and just got a new boat."

I handed over her cup of coffee. Apparently Kathy has figured out our weekly meetings and the sustenance required. "This is good. You can spend the day in the boat, thinking about your next chapter. It'll give you a chance to think like your reader."

"See, your reader will eventually go fishing as well—at least metaphorically, which means they can't read your book through in one sitting. And, just like you as the author need to keep the momentum going between chapters as you write, you also need think about keeping the momentum going between the chapters for the reader. You do this by using, just to keep with the fishing theme, a "bait and hook" technique. Or better…a Hook and Bait technique."

Sally raised an eyebrow.

"Think of it like this—every chapter—every scene, really–has to start with a hook, something that will make the reader want to read the chapter. Think if it as something at stake, or something the character is risking in the scene. We talked about this over the past month as we talked about Scene tension and rhythm. But in essence, the magic of the character setting a goal and then the author threatening that goal through conflict is what hooks the reader into the scene/chapter. However, when they get to the end of the chapter, the tension is over....and the reader has a choice. Put the book down or keep reading.

"You want them to keep reading. You do this by baiting them on to the next scene by raising a new problem. Giving them a glimpse of trouble. Think of a soap opera for a moment. They end the scenes—even the happy ones—with a sense of, 'Uh oh! If Jane only knew. Or, wait until she realizes that Bob is a serial killer. Or, Joe is still alive? Or, that's Rachel's evil twin he's kissing!' Something that whets our appetite for more.

"We talked about this a few Conversations ago when we addressed Scene Rhythm. The Action scene must end with a disaster that contributes to the overall Black Moment event, and causes the character to have to make a decision about his next course of action. We often call this the Y in the road for the character, but it's also the key to keeping your reader turning pages.

"Again, think of the ending as Bait. How will you make the reader hunger for more? It's not just about ending with a new problem— it must be a compelling and preferably timely problem that needs to be addressed...well, right now by the reader."

I heard a honk outside. Sally made a face. "Speaking of right now..." She got up, taking her coffee.

"Maybe you'll get a tan."

Truth: A great page turner not only hooks the reader at the beginning of each chapter, but baits them at the end of each chapter with a compelling problem that forces them to turn the page.

Dare: Look at your chapter endings. Have you created new problems for your character, or are all their problems solved? Don't let your reader fall asleep!

Quick Skills: Scene Creation Steps Summary

Part One

Keeping Scene Momentum: Character Journal

Ask the following questions of your character:

1. What did you think about what just happened?

2. What are your choices?

3. What will you do next and why?

4. What is the worst thing that could happen to you right now?

5. And, if it's a romance –how do you feel about this person? What do you fear happening emotionally?

Part Two

Create Scene Tension

Scene Tension Equation: Sympathetic Character + Stakes + Goals + Obstacles + Fear of Failure

Step 1: Determine your Action Objectives

What kind of scene is it?

Action: Goal, Conflict, Disaster

Reaction: Response, Dilemma, Decision

Ask: What does POV want? What does he/she want at this moment? Emotionally, physically? Answering this question will help you build the conflict.

Add in:

Why do they want this?

What is the Push/Pull?

Every scene has to have an emotional or physical Push/Pull (or combination thereof). It's the Push away from something negative, and the Pull toward something positive.

- What's at Stake: What will happen if they *don't* meet their goal?
- What fear hovers over the scene?

What is your character's Goal? This may be different from the Want, but be driven by the Want and the Why.

Step 2: What are the Obstacles?

Step 3: Create a Fear of Failure

Will your character reach thier goal?

If not, then hint that they will in the scene, make them believe they'll have victory, only to disappoint them at the end.

If yes, then hint that they will fail, only to surprise them at the end.

Step 4: Start On the Run!

Start with the character already in the scene. Can you move your character five minutes later into the scene?

Step 5: Create Sympathy

Is your character doing something sympathetic? Something that makes us care about her? Are her emotions realistic?

Step 6: Where do you start? (Build the 5 Ws/Facts)

Start with the basics—the five Ws. Who, What, Where, Why, When. The reader needs to know who is in the scene, where it is, when it is, what is going on around the character, and a little about why they're there.

Ask:

> Who—Who are the players in the scene? (And how do they feel about being there?)
>
> Where—What details stand out to the character? Why is this significant to the character?
>
> When is it—What is the time of year, and how do we know that? (we're again looking for details here.)
>
> What—What other activities are going on in the scene? What is your POV character doing?
>
> Why—Why is she/he in this place?

Part Three

▸ Find your First Line/First Paragraph

> What are the Stakes?
>
> How will you create Sympathy for your character (Hero/Heroine ID)?
>
> Are you starting with a sympathetic situation?
>
> Are you starting with a relatable emotion?
>
> How will you Anchor your reader into the scene with Storyworld? (Hint: Sight, Smell, Sound, Touch, Taste)
>
> Are you starting your scene On the Run—with the scene already in motion?
>
> What Problem/Story Question will your character deal with?
>
> Set the Hook by asking: What is my character thinking right now? How can I express this in a statement, question, action, or determination?

Part Four

End with Bait for the next chapter. How can I raise a new problem or an "Uh Oh" that compels my reader to turn the page?

Quick Skill: It helps to talk through these steps with a craft partner. Take notes…and then sit down and write!

Conversation #22: The Basics of Building Storyworld

Dear Sally,

I'm thinking of you sitting in our coffee shop, the hush of the waves of Lake Superior combing the shore, the sky so blue you could dive in, the smell of evergreen fresh in the air from last night's rain. But I'm writing to you from the beaches of Hawaii, my toes dug into the creamy sand, the salt of the ocean drying into crystals on my skin.

As you're diving into your novel and writing scenes, I thought it might help if we touched upon Storyworld this week. Storyworld is so key, from the first scene to every scene beyond, to anchor your character—and especially your reader—into the story.

Think of Storyworld as more than just the setting. It's the world you wrap your reader into as you tell the story. The facts, the five senses, the dialogue, the culture—everything that makes up the world of your novel.

Great storyworld contains the **DETAILS**. It's the rich combination of all the elements that go into the world of the scene.

Here's how it breaks down:

1. **Dress**—It's not what color gown she wears, but why she is wearing the gown. It's not whether he wears a suit, but what kind of suit, or tux. The reader wants to see the character, but don't throw your character into any old outfit—pick their clothes carefully, to betray their goals and their attitudes and intentions for the scene.

I am a fan of fantasy novels because they are masters of storyworld. They have to be to help us see the speculative world they invite us into. Consider how, in *The Hunger Games*, every detail of Katniss's entrance into the arena, including her attire, is essential to building the story.

Be specific and thoughtful with your character's costuming.

2. **Environment**—This is more than the setting. It's the season, and the place, and the architecture. Stories set in New York should note the garbage laying on the streets in July, and the beauty of Central Park in September. They should include the smell of the subway and the noise it makes as it rushes into the station with a shudder that the character can feel to their bones. Stories set in Montana should note the trailer houses, the rough-cut terrain covered with bramble, the undulating fence lines that ride over gully and knoll, and if it is in winter, the patches of gray snow, the brown-yellow grass, the trails of hay that beckon the cattle. Make it real, and use finite details to bring your reader into the world of the character.

3. **Time Period**—Even if it is a contemporary novel, you can build in the faces, music, and norms of the time. If it is a historical novel, be lavish with the nuances of the culture. Do your research to discover things unknown to most readers. It will make their reading even richer. This also includes influences of movies, books, political figures—anything to help build the appropriate time period for your world.

4. **Attitudes**—Insert the attitudes of the place, culture, setting, time period. What social circle does your character run in? What would be normal for him to say, do, allow, think? How about those around him? Dropping clues through dialogue, dress, or action

about the prevailing attitudes of the world of your story will help your reader understand the situation and motivations of your character.

5. Inferences or Expectations—Think about the things in your life that you "expect." Your Internet to work. Your cell phone to ring. Your character will have things he/she expects to happen—and writing that expectation into the scene will help it flow, and keep the reader in story world. What do I mean? Let's say you're writing a Biblical fiction. Going to the well for daily water would be an expectation. It would be normal, everyday life. You wouldn't expound on it like you've never done it before. Another common way to say this is R.U.E. (Resist the urge to explain).

"Rachael searched for the wooden bucket that she always used to fetch water, which she did every morning. It had a rough handle, and she hated how it dug into her hand when she lugged home the family's water, although she was careful not to spill it. She had done that yesterday, and earned a beating."

That's a lot of information, and probably something your character wouldn't think. Instead, infer the expectation that she goes to the well, simplify the details, focusing on the most vivid, and most profound.

"The rough handle gouged her hands as she trudged back from the well, but she bit back her pain and held the water bucket out from her body. Mamma would be furious if she spilled it, again. Her back still ached from yesterday's beating."

6. Language—Every place, time period, social strata, and even age group has their own language. Utilize it to illuminate the world they live in. A great example of this is, of course, Eliza and Henry Higgins, from *My Fair Lady*. I'm always amazed at the transformation right before our eyes of Eliza as she begins to speak proper English. Language is a powerful tool for Storyworld (as well as characterization). Don't let your Scottish warrior sound like an Englishman from Parliament. Or your Bostonian like a Minnesotan! I know an editor who has fits when modern-day young adult characters talk and act like senior citizens. Remember who your characters are!

7. **Senses**—I know I'm constantly harping on you to use the five senses when writing a scene but use your five senses! Don't just tell us what it looks like! The five senses help the reader enter Story-world with your hero. Don't leave him staring through a window, unable to experience more than just seeing his world.

• Those seven points spell the word...DETAILS. (You know how I like my acronyms!) And that's what Storyworld is. It's specific nouns, and rich (yet sparing) adjectives, and vivid verbs. It's taking the time to build your world around your hero.

For your homework this week, create scenes set in modern day New York, World War II London and somewhere in the Wild West. Can you write the correct storyworld?

See you next week, same time, same coffee shop.

Fondly,

Susie May

Truth: An author has to step out of their world and into the world of their character to write authentic Storyworld.

Dare: Pick a character in history, or current, someone outside your current world and write a scene or storyworld description in their voice. Don't name the location and give it to a reader. Can they name the location?

Conversation #23: How to build POV into your Storyworld

Sally tossed her notebook on the table. "You're tan. How fair is that? I'm still pasty white."

I gave her a smile. "I'm still the underside of a walleye compared to the Hawaiians, not to mention the native Hawaiians.... How is your storyworld writing going?"

"It feels like a travel brochure. I don't know how to make it interesting."

"It's all about perspective, which is what I want to talk to you about today. Every book, regardless of what kind—Suspense/Romance, Fantasy, Thriller, Historical romance—every book starts out someplace. In a world. At a moment. And, in today's literature, with a person. Whether it's a firecracker start to a book, or something that begins with a wide-angle view drawing the reader into the scene, the world is viewed through the eyes of a character.

"It's the perspective of this character that gives the storyworld life.

"One of my favorite novels, *Wiser than Serpents*, started in the night market, in Taiwan. I could have started with description: the hundreds of tables pushed side by side, the vendors hawking chicken legs and squid on a stick, the cloying smell of sweet potatoes mixed with the pungency of tea eggs. I could have talked about the voices of the vendors, each rising above the other in a wild, chaotic cacophony that outshouted even the seagulls at the nearby shipyards.

However, if I simply describe the scene, then the reader doesn't know how to interpret what they see. They need a character to perceive the sights and sift them through their grid of understanding. Scenery without POV interpretation is, well, boring. (Unless it's in omniscient pov, but then again, you do have a POV — the narrator).

"And it's not just the POV that matters, but what is at stake for the POV character that turns the setting into something vibrant and distinct. What if the character was looking for a small boy, lost in the crowd? Every vendor would be suspect, every vat of boiling oil a horror.

"Or, what if he was hiding from someone? Suddenly the market becomes his salvation. What if he's hungry and has no money? Then the night market becomes tantalizing, and perhaps pushes him over the edge.

"Here's the secret—move your character through the scene, experiencing the world as they go, wrapping it up in their attitudes and stakes. The scene will go from static to alive."

I pulled out a book and opened it. "This is one of my scenes in *Wiser than Serpents*. It is written from the POV of the hero. See if you can pinpoint the way his attitudes are woven through the scene to give it more life."

> He'd never eaten deep fried frog on a stick, but David Curtiss was a patriot, and he'd do just about anything for his country.
>
> "Shei Shei," he said as he took the delicacy from the vendor, fished out a New Taiwan Dollar, and dropped it into the vendor's hand.
>
> He wondered what might leave a worse taste in his mouth, fried frog, or meeting a man who had beheaded the two undercover agents that had tried this trick before David. But if all

went as planned, his culinary sacrifice would lead him to the identity of Kwan-Li, leader of the Twin Serpents, the largest organized crime syndicate in eastern Asia.

The smells of night market were enough to turn even his iron gut to mush — body odor, eggs boiled in soy sauce, fresh fish and oil redolent from the nearby shipyard. Even worse, the fare offered in the busy open market sounded like something from a house of horrors menu: Grilled chicken feet, boiled snails, breaded salamander, poached pigeon eggs, and the specialty of the day — carp head soup.

"What did you get me into, Chet?" he whispered, wondering if Chet Stryker, his co-hort for this unfortunate op, was grinning at the other end of his transmitter. "Squid, or even snails, okay, but a frog?" Chet had set up this meet — and the frog signal. "Next time, you're going to be drinking asparagus juice, buddy." He hoped Chet's silence meant he still had eyes on him. David hadn't seen his partner in the forty-five minutes he'd been walking around the market — a sign of Chet's skill, no doubt.

David looked at the brown and crispy frog and wondered if he was supposed to add condiments —he'd noticed a sort of ketchup, and horseradish at the bar.

A few more seconds and he'd have to take a bite. It wasn't enough to just stand here and try to blend with the crowd — not an easy task given that every man who brushed by him stood around chin height. Even with David's long black dyed hair, silk Asian shirt, and designer jeans, he knew he looked like a walking American billboard. Thankfully, foreigners flocked to the novelty of night market in this part of Kaohsiung in Taiwan.

He saw a couple of Americans stroll by, listened to their comments about the food, the smells. A short blonde, slightly pudgy, wearing a blue Taiwanese shirt and shorts set probably purchased in a local beach shop sucked on the straw of a Ju Ju Bee shake. Next to her, her husband was finishing off a grilled squid. Aid workers, probably — the island had a plethora of Americans working in relief and humanitarian aid agencies. Especially after the last earthquake.

He checked his watch. Kwan's man was late. Which meant he'd have to take a bite of froggie.

He lifted the amphibian to his mouth.

I closed the book.

"Everything that happens in night market is through David's eyes, as he's waiting for his contact. Because it's a thriller, I go right into the action, but I still want readers to know where they are.

"Creating storyworld is more than just an overview of scenery. It's details, and the perspective of the character in it.

"Ask: What will my character see/care about as he walks into the scene? How will that be reflected in the way he sees the scene?

"So, give your character something to care about, something to do, and then drop them into the world and write the scene through their eyes."

Sally shrugged. "I think I might understand this much better if next year you took me to Hawaii with you."

Truth: Great storyworld isn't simply a description of the world—it must happen through the POV of your character— including thier fears, opinions, and delights.

Dare: Go to a location and write a description of the scene through the eyes of three different characters (you might also do this with a description of a person!).

Conversation #24: How to use storyworld to build emotions in a scene

A glorious blue sky beckoned me onto the porch of the coffee shop where a light summer breeze rustled the impatiens in the containers, the tangy scent of deep-fried donuts scenting the air. I took a sip of coffee, waiting for Sally, watching the lazy caress of the waves upon the rocky shoreline, listening to gulls cheering on the tourists.

Today, I would talk to Sally about using storyworld to build emotions. A great story is about connecting with the reader at an emotional level. We want them to feel what the character feels and thus engage in their experience on the page.

Storyworld helps build the emotional engagement. How? With the right use of nouns and verbs, and the way they are woven together, the reader receives an impression, even if it's a subtle one, about the mood of the scene.

We had talked last week about POV affecting how someone describes a location. Their mood, reason for being there, and even focus affects how they describe the place.

Now she needed a foundation to build emotions into the scene. Once she determined how her POV character felt, she could begin to embed these emotions into the scene, subtly, using the right nuance of words.

I pulled out the example I would show her. In this scene, which was a sunny bright day, I wanted to hint at danger lurking in the caves and contrast it with the recklessness of Dino. I wanted her to notice the verbs and nouns I use to infer this. (This excerpt is taken from *Sons of Thunder*, which won a 2011 Carol Award).

Lucien then disappeared, of course, into the maw of the white-washed caves that tumbled from the cliffs straight into the sea.

Indeed, the sea beckoned, the azure blue nearly hypnotic with its lure, and on a different day, Markos, too, might have surrendered to the chase. After all, he'd been bred for the taste of salt on his chapped lips.

Not today. "Lucien!"

Dino stepped up, a bare foot curled around the edge of the boat.

"Dino—you're not going after him. You're not strong enough—the waves will smash you against the opening."

"I'm not afraid, Markos."

Markos put warning into his eyes. "It's too dangerous."

How Markos hated Whistler's Drink.

Even if Dino managed to swim into the puckered lips of the cavern, the cave had already begun to fill and soon would engulf the escape, perhaps purge any air supply from the deep veins inside. Moreover, once inside, the cauldron could grab Dino's lanky body and thrash it against the rocks. Worse, legend spoke of tunnels that channeled inland, emerged into the lush olive groves overlooking the city, and enticed young divers to lose their lives in the twisted channels.

"I know he went into the caves—I'm going after him." Dino poised now on the boat's rim, one hand on the mast for balance, his eyes shining.

"No."

"I'll be right back!" As slick as a sardine, Dino sliced the water, a clean dive to the bottom of the sea.

"Dino!" But the boy was a fish, and slipped away, toward the overhanging tongue of rock that lapped the water.

I also had another scene, from the same book. It was a scene into which I wanted to insert the feeling of desire and temptation.

"Hedy, how long have you known Jimmy?"

Markos sat facing the door, inside the cramped quarters of her private dressing room at the Blue Moon. The place swam with her perfume, the cloying smell of a woman's clothing. He'd wanted to park himself outside, in the hallway, but Jimmy had come by that first night, seen him loitering on the wrong side of her door, and nearly took off his head.

Now, he just tried not to glance in the mirror, where the bright bulbs illuminated her array of makeup pots, jewelry, and discarded headdresses. Or the hosiery that hung over the top of the dressing screen.

"See how I use a strong image, almost like her legs hanging over the top?"

In yet another scene, I wanted to draw out the sense of fatigue and being overwhelmed, as Dino (a doctor) tells his brother that one of his men died.

"Please tell me Private Burke is alive." Markos sat propped against the rocky wall, away from the chaos of the courtyard, his fingers in a can of C-rations—what might be beef stew but looked just as appetizing as one of the muddy bogs indenting the French countryside. Smoke bit the air, the glow from burning houses or tires pulsing against the night. In the courtyard, men smoked cigarettes, coughing, slapping at mosquitoes. Firelight lit their faces, brutal shadows hollowing their eyes.

Dino stared at his clean hands, at the way they shook. Fisted them. "I'm sorry, Markos. He was in bad shape."

And in this final scene, I wanted to show the sense of danger and fear of the German presence in their Greek island.

The wind scraped from the wooden dock the briny odor of fish and seaweed, rustled the grove of calamus reeds along the shore. She pulled her knitted sweater tighter over her thin cotton dress, the air having turned cool with the desertion of the sun. Gooseflesh raised on her arms. Somewhere in the darkness, waves knocked against the bright red hulls of fishing boats tied up at the long piers in the bay. Farther out, the beady lights of a German transport peered into the starless night.

A spotlight sliced through the night from the hilltop overlooking the city, sliding over the faraway cliffs, the blue cupolas of the Greek Orthodox churches, the tall bell tower, the whitewashed homes that flowed up the mountainside, between Cyprus, and willows, aspen, and poplar. What had been a village exploded into a small city over her ten-year absence, and she'd donned a black scarf and slipped back into her life, her scars folded neatly inside.

Now, she pressed herself against the building, even as footsteps shuffled toward her.

"Sofia?"

As an author describes the world of thier characters, every word adds nuance to the mood of the scene. Figure out the emotion you want to convey and build it into the background by the subtle use of strong verbs and nouns, the occasional symbolic image.

Sally came up on the porch, holding a blended coffee, whipped cream spilling down the sides. She dropped her bag on the deck, plunked herself down in an Adirondack chair, put her feet up on the bench, closed her eyes.

"You just let me know when you want to start working," I said.

Truth: Every word counts in your story, and the way you weave your storyworld can create an emotional backdrop and add the first emotional layer to your scene.

Dare: Edit a scene, first identifying the emotion, and then honing your verbs and nouns to create a powerful backdrop.

Quick Skills: Bringing Storyworld to Life with the 5 senses

I am a "List and Schedule" girl—I like to have a checklist when I build a scene to make sure I've inserted everything into it that will give it the strongest emotional impact.

One of these checklists, and something commonly missed, are the five senses. To really draw your Storyworld, you need to use your five senses to engage the reader's emotions. **Sight. Smell. Sound. Touch. Taste.** When you walk into a room, all your senses are a part of your understanding of that scene.

Before you sit down to write, make a sensory list of everything you perceive in that scene. You'll use it as a "cheat sheet" as you build the scene.

Sight, of course, is what a scene is usually built on, but remember those specific, mood-enhancing details.

Smell: It's a huge memory tool, and, just like you, your character will remember scents and/or odors.

How do you write about a smell?

How it makes you feel: nauseating, intoxicating, making our stomach turn over, etc.

You can describe it in terms of other smells—"like" comparisons

(Think like a perfumer. Minty. Floral. Earthy. Or a wine taster. Nutty, fruity, oaky.)

Confine the smell to a place or time: The jovial freshness of the Fourth of July, grilled hotdogs, cinnamon apple pie, and the tangy sweetness of a bomb pop.

And you can combine them all:

The prunes turned my stomach over even before I saw them, a dark, oily mass that stenched the room with the pungent odor of engine grease and hickory coals, and conjured up images of my uncle's dirt-floored garage behind his house.

I encourage all my students to familiarize themselves with scent words: Musty, sweaty, sickly sweet, acrid, pungent…

Sound: Rarely is there a place without some noise in it, yet we often don't read about it or hear it in a scene. Imagine watching a movie with the sound off—this is what happens when you don't put sound into a book. Sound, probably more than anything, can bring a scene to life.

The wind from this black—sometimes green— sea moaned in his ears, burned his throat.

Around him, the foreign syllables gnawed at his ears.

The whistle blew, a high shrill that never failed to make him wince.

I've used a couple different techniques here:

State the sound directly: The whistle blew. We understand what that sounds like.

Give it a surprising modifier:

The wind moaned in his ears. (verb)

The Voice raked over him like a storm wave, gritty, cold, even violent as it turned him. (simile)

The buzzing turned into a hum, then a rumble as Dino found his feet, propped his hands over his eyes. Two Stukas dropped from the clouds, set on a course for the hospital. (adjectives)

Give it context—tell how it is heard:

Markos would know the song anywhere, but especially the way it lifted above the rush of the waves, more like a feeling than a tune, seasoned with the tang of the sea, the jangle of goats' bells in the far off hills.

Use Onomatopoeia effect—help us to feel the sound by reproducing the sound on the page. (not ring ring goes the phone).

The sound of bedroom slippers moving on carpet might be the hush of slippers, or the whisper of slippers.

A deep thrumming rumbled his bones...

The thunderous gulp of the cave...

Help us to hear it.

Touch: We touch people and things every day. The sense of touch is about slowing the act down for us to feel it, to recognize it, and to give an emotional component. Your character can rub her hand on the soft, worn leather of a desk chair or dig her fingers into the rough bark of an oak tree.

Shards of ice cut his skin even as he lay there, breathing in blades of air.

Markos speared the water. The cool lick of it scooped his breath, slicked from his body the heat of the day.

The kind of chill he couldn't flee pressed into his bones, turned him brittle.

The touch should connect us emotionally to the scene, and to the description.

Taste: We taste things in our memory. Your heroine could taste her fear. She tasted her past, the memory of sitting in the kitchen with her mother, sneaking cookie dough out of the bowl.

This works in conjunction with smell as a memory element.

You can use taste two ways: Literally and Figuratively

Literally: Say what it is: Sweet, sour, bitter, salty.

Tell the effect of it.....the sweetly bitter chocolate dissolved in my mouth, flooding every cranny until my eyes rolled back in my head.

Attach the taste to a memory: The taste of my grandmother's kitchen, her chocolate chip cookies fresh out of the freezer, better licked than crunched, the sweetness slicking off onto our eager tongues, dissolving into our mouths as we grinned chocolate.

Figuratively: We can taste fear, joy, hope, love.

She could taste their tomorrows in his kiss.

You can slurp up the salty air of the ocean, or drink in a tangy summer evening. The innocence of a baby's skin, the taste of hot fever in a concert hall.

"Is there a radio in here?"

The voice roused him as he lay on his side, wedged into the short length of the spongy lounge davenport. His neck screamed when he pushed to a sitting position, the hot seams of the vinyl drawn into his face. His mouth tasted as if he'd chewed on cotton batting.

A great scene has all five senses embedded in a way that adds emotional nuance.

Quick Skill: Write your scene, and then, in the rewrite, meticulously craft in the five senses, adding the subtle emotional layers.

3½

Conversation #25: Subtexting and the powerful flow of dialogue

"My husband is driving me crazy." Sally sat down on the Adirondack chair on the deck of the coffee shop, facing the lake. She turned her chair to the morning sun, lifted her face to it, closed her eyes. "I just want to sit here and not talk."

I raised an eyebrow. "Did you have a nice visit to your mother-in-law's house this weekend?"

She opened an eye. "My husband and I rode home in two-and-a-half hours of stony silence."

"Ah," I said. "Silence that speaks a thousand words. A form of dialogue in itself, which is what I wanted to talk to you about today."

"How is silence a form of dialogue?"

"I'm certain you communicated, even if you didn't use words, right?"

She made a face.

I laughed. "Great dialogue raises conflict and contains subtexting about the deeper issues of the story."

"I've heard of subtexting, but I have no idea what that is."

"Subtexting is the foundation of all great dialogue, and what makes it really come to life. Everything you say, how you say it, what you do with your body language, and even internal monologue has meaning. Which means that behind every conversation is a bigger message, a deeper meaning.

"Subtexting is the meaning behind the words, what the characters are really communicating by their tone of voice, their body language, their internal thought, even the precision of their words to mean something else. As you build your dialogue, Subtexting will embed every word your characters utter."

"You mean that everything we say has a double meaning?"

"No. Everything we say has a deeper meaning, expressed in what is said, or not said, in the meaningful action or body language, and in the tones we use. We're going to talk this month about all these elements of dialogue.

"First, however, let's take a look at how dialogue actually works. When an author is creating dialogue, often it comes out as two people having a mundane conversation. We're going to solve that problem by adding some tricks and techniques, but let's start by understanding the rhythm and flow of dialogue. Many times the problem with stalled dialogue is simply because the author has forgotten an important step in the flow."

I picked up a rock that I'd stolen from the beach and tossed it out into the water. Ripples surrounded the place where it landed. "I like to think of great dialogue as a rock landing in water. It all starts with one drop. That drop starts the dialogue and it causes a ripple effect.

"This is the important missing step in so much dialogue…the way the character interprets the first 'stone' thrown. Consider every powerful conversation you've ever had—was it the words that made it impactful, or was it the way you interpreted what was said? Every character involved in the dialogue will interpret the words in a different way, based on their goals, needs, wants, and fears.

"Imagine a character says something innocuous, but the second character interprets what they say negatively. Perhaps their feelings are hurt. Perhaps they are angered. Now, they have a choice. They can either react to the words…or not. When they don't react at all, then you lose your opportunity for powerful dialogue. But if they react, the ripples continue."

"The reaction might even be non-verbal dialogue, like when I slowly reach for my door handle when my husband is driving too fast," Sally said. "That starts a few ripples."

"Exactly, because he interprets your 'communication' as criticism, and then reacts to his interpretation."

"If he didn't react, then it wouldn't escalate into a fight as we travel down the highway."

"Indeed. In powerful dialogue, the interpretation is followed by a Reaction. Preferably in dialogue, although it can be in body language or meaningful action also. The Reaction will be guided by the goals of the characters as well as the things they fear. And the cycle continues. The second character interprets the response of the first character, reacts, and the conversation continues. And it doesn't have to be a fight—it might be a highly emotional revelation. Or a moment of vulnerability. But it's all based on this rhythm of dialogue—interpretation—response.

"Subtexting is how you build in meaning behind the response—in tone, word, or action. It's also when you talk about one thing and mean another, like a word picture, or metaphorical speech. In short, subtexting is everything behind the words that add the deeper level of meaning.

"Your homework this week is to search for subtexted speech in your conversations. But try not to pick a fight."

She sighed.

"I think that's enough subtexting for today," I said. "I'll go get you a Frappucino."

Truth—Great dialogue is not conversation, but contrived conversation with all the mundanc bits deleted. And it always contains a deeper meaning, called subtexting.

Dare—What are your characters really trying to say? Pick up a passage of dialogue and search for the subtexting—it might surprise you!

Conversation #26: Adding Punch to your dialogue by creating Meaningful Action

"You look upset," Sally said as she sat down on the deck. She wore a white shirt, her hair pulled back in a sixties' style headband, and she sported a sleek summer tan.

I sighed, stirring my blended mocha. "I just had a difficult conversation with my son about his driving skills."

"Did you argue?"

"No. And that's the problem. He said everything right. It's what he didn't say that bothered me."

She frowned.

"I was driving, he was riding beside me when I broached the topic. I mentioned that we'd seen him driving in town recently a little too recklessly, and if he wanted to drive our cars he'd have to slow down."

"And?"

"He said, 'Sure, Mom. Whatever.'"

"That doesn't sound–"

"He was scrolling through his music on his iTouch at the time. As soon as he said it, he plugged in his earphones and cranked on some screamer music. He then stared out the window the entire ride as if I didn't exist."

"Oh," she said.

"Technically, his words said he agreed. But his body language and actions screamed dissent." I took a sip of my frap. "That's what I wanted to talk about today—how dialogue is accentuated by the action that surrounds it.

"Of course, your dialogue is the primary vehicle for your conversation. However, like we talked about last week, every conversation has a meaning behind it, and there is always subtexting going on, either in words –meaning they have double meaning—or in actions. In this case, my son displayed by his actions—louder than his words — that he didn't want to hear my criticism. Great dialogue employs the combination of words plus meaningful action plus body language to create a powerful impact.

"Meaningful action is just that—an action beyond body language that adds another layer of meaning to your dialogue. When we are in a scene, just to have your characters reacting with their facial expressions or tone makes for a mundane scene. A person can only smile so much, right?"

She smiled, nodded.

"So, you want to wrap up their words in actions that can deepen their meaning, like my son did when he plugged in his earphones."

Sally reached into her bag. "So, when I consider my dialogue, I have to also think through what my character is doing while he's speaking and use that to add meaning to the scene." She pulled out a notebook and opened it on her lap.

"Exactly. It doesn't work with every scene—especially if it's a big argument. Because frankly, you don't need it then, but for those medium tension scenes, add in some meaningful action and a touch of body language, and you just might have the reader stewing all day. Your homework for the week is to find a ho-hum scene and add some meaningful action."

She leaned over. "Here's a meaningful action. Make him pay for his insurance, and he'll turn off that iTouch, I'll bet."

I grinned and held up my drink in a toast. "Sally, you're a genius."

Truth: To power up your dialogue, add meaningful action and only a scant amount of body language.

Dare: Go through a scene and take out all the instances of tone of voice and facial expression. Can you insert a strong, meaningful action instead?

Conversation #27: How to make your dialogue pop!

"It's so hot, I think I'm melting. I haven't been able to write for three days." Sally held a cold vanilla mocha, sweat glistening on her forehead as she plunked down on the Adirondack chair next to me.

"Really? What, has your brain turned to mush? Are your fingers slipping off the keyboard?"

She stared at me, frowning. "Ouch."

"If you want to be a writer, Sally, you have to press on. Do you want to be a writer? Or just a wannabe?"

"I think I'm going to take my mocha elsewhere."

"There's no crying in writing, bay-bee. I once wrote a book while living in a garage without plumbing, heat, or electricity. Believe me, I had reasons not to write. You have to press on, like a mailman, through sleet and snow and dead of night."

"But—"

"No buts!"

She closed her mouth, considered me for a moment.

I smiled. "I'm just trying to teach you how to put zingers into your dialogue."

"Zingers?"

"They are my Super Secret Susie tricks to adding spice to your dialogue. Sarcasm, Accusations, Interruptions, Name Calling."

"I don't think your zingers are very nice."

"But they do add drama to a conversation, right? By the way, it's been too hot for me to write, also. I read a book for the past three days." I winked at her.

She smiled. "Okay, I get it. Zingers are those devices I can insert into dialogue to take it a new direction."

"Or add spark to it. Polite, boring conversation has no drama. Drama is found in the unexpected, the uncouth, the ugly. Let's take a standard conversation, one that I hear at my house quite often.

"'Can I get a ride to work today?' my son said as he emerged from his room in uniform.

"'I'll be happy to drive you,' I said, grabbing the keys.

Let's add some drama to this.

Accusation:

"'Can I get a ride to work today?'"

"'Don't you think it's about time you bought your own wheels? What are you doing with all that money you're earning at Dairy Queen?'"

Interruption:

"'Can I get a —'"

"'Oh no, you're not asking for a ride again, are you?'"

Name Calling:

"'Can I get a ride to work today?'"

"'Sure, Your Highness.'"

Sarcasm:

"'Can I get a ride to work today?'"

"'Absolutely, Son, because I see your legs no longer work.'"

"See, all these little zingers add spark to your dialogue and have the potential to take the dialogue in a new direction, or add depth. They are a great tool to use if you feel your dialogue is becoming mundane. That's your homework this week—to find a passage of dialogue and add a zinger. Better, find a few and try out different zingers and see what happens."

Sally took a sip of her drink. Then, "You really know how to pick a fight, don't you?"

"I have teenagers, what can I say?"

Truth: To create spark in your dialogue, you might want to fight dirty and throw in a few zingers.

Dare: Do you have a piece of mundane dialogue? Try adding a zinger to your piece and see how it causes sparks and perhaps even takes it deeper, to the real meaning behind the dialogue.

5/2

Conversation #28: "I'd thought she'd never get here." (The powerful use of internal monologue)

Sally shot me a look as she sat down on the Adirondack chair next to me. She eyed me warily. "Were you talking to me?"

"No. Why would you think that?" I paused, looked away. "She's so paranoid."

"Are you schizophrenic?" She raised an eyebrow. "I'm sitting right here."

"Sheesh, touchy," I said softly. Then, "What are you talking about? How are you?" I smiled.

She stared at me like I'd turned purple. I laughed. "I was internal monologueing."

"Out loud?"

"So you could hear it."

"Please tell me that's not what you really think. I didn't mean to be late—"

"Calm down, Sally, it was just for teaching purposes. But if you were reading that, it would certainly add a bit of tension to the scene, right?"

"I know I feel a little tense."

"I just wanted to touch one last time on Dialogue before we started talking about showing and telling. It's hard to know how to use Internal Monologue and Tone of Voice for maximum impact, so I thought I would try and explain.

"Internal monologue is about what the POV character is thinking—wishing they could say, but can't."

"Or shouldn't," she said, sipping her coffee.

"Right. It's the secrets they really can't put to rest, or the voices in their head that are reminding them of past conversations."

"Like if my internal monologue went something like, 'Sheesh, if she says one more thing, I might just get up and walk away.'"

"Right. But please, don't. Instead, ask yourself: What is my character thinking right now, and how does it influence what he/she says next? Remember, when you're in Deep POV, your internal monologue should be in third person, past tense (if your story is in past tense).

"The answer to that question will influence not only what they say next, but how they say it. In other words, it may mean you need to interject a tone of voice."

"What's a tone of voice?"

"Something that indicates how the character said it. He whispered. His voice cut low. She yelled. She snapped. In a perfect world, an author should never have to really use a tone of voice, because the words speak for themselves. However, when your character raises or lowers their voice, perhaps they snap at someone or even shout, then that may call for a dialogue tone-of-voice tag.

"Be very frugal with your use of tone of voice, and it will carry great impact."

"Why," she whispered. "Doesn't it make it more interesting to hear how they say it?"

"People change their tone of voice to make a point, or add drama to a conversation. Imagine doing that for every line—not only does turn ridiculous, but it loses its impact."

"Fine, she snapped," Sally said.

"Oh brother. Just do me this favor. Remember the rhythm of dialogue: Goal—Dialogue—Interpretation—Reaction—Goal.

"When you write dialogue, if you start with the Action Objectives and Goals of your character, and follow the rhythm of interpretation, reaction, and goal, then you will write dialogue that makes sense as well as increases the conflict. Don't forget to put in some powerful zingers, and use internal monologue and tone of voice correctly and sparingly. Finally, backdrop it all with body language and meaningful action that symbolizes the character's feelings, desires or unspoken words.

"Once you've done that, take a look at the entire passage. What is the real meaning behind what they are saying? How can you enhance it, ever so slightly, to draw out the meaning? Can you add a tone of voice—or perhaps even delete dialogue and simply let the meaningful action speak for itself? Don't highlight it or it will feel over the top, as if you are hitting the reader over the head. Keep it light, simple and yet profound. This is how you will create powerful subtexted dialogue."

"Aye, aye, Captain."

"She said, right before her teacher dumped her smoothie in her lap."

Truth: Internal Monologue, used correctly, and Tone of Voice, used sparingly, can add depth to your dialogue.

Dare: After you're finished with a passage of dialogue, review it. Ask: What is the real meaning behind what they are saying? Can you enhance it through tone of voice, meaningful action, or even internal dialogue? This will help you create subtexted dialogue.

Quick Skills: A Conversation about Italics and Internal Monologue

Italics and Internal Monologue can be very confusing. I write in Deep POV, so for those who employ this technique, here are some hints that might help.

If you're writing in Deep POV, which is common for today's authors, remember that you're in a character's pov, so anything they think, feel, see, or hear filters through their head and directly onto the page. Thus, if it doesn't have quotation marks around it, it is internal and should not be in italics.

The only time you need italics is when the character is remembering another voice in their head, or they are unable to voice the words they are thinking. For example, if a person is remembering something their mother or their pastor or their friend said, or even something they read, it is another "Voice" in their head and goes into italics. Likewise, if they are watching someone leave from across the room and are unable to say, Stop, don't go! all the while screaming it in their head—that also would follow the italic rule.

Think of internal monologue set in italics as a memory or another voice speaking inside your POV character's head and you'll get it right.

Now that the italic issue is settled, here are my rules of thumb when using internal monologue:

If your story is in third person, the italics should be in third person.

Consider this thought inside a third person passage.

"Nick watched from his office window as Rachel tore open her car door and threw herself inside. *I really don't want her to leave, because if she does leave I'll be alone and back where I started.*"

This thought feels jarring for the reader, because it's in first person.

Try: Nick watched from his office window as Rachel tore open her car door and threw herself inside. He didn't want her to leave. Not really. *Because then where would he be?*

Do you see the difference? Third person keeps us in the correct tense and in the POV character's thought.

When writing in deep third POV, this rule applies to notations like "He thought" or "He wondered." You know who is thinking the thought, so it's not necessary.

Incorrect: Did he really want her to leave? *No,* he thought.

Try: Did he really want her to leave? *No.*

Incorrect: *He always took a good thing and tore it to pieces,* he thought about himself.

Try: *He always took a good thing and tore it to pieces.*

And you can give it even more impact by converting interior monologue into a question.

He wondered why he always took a good thing and tore it to pieces.

Better: *Why did he always take a good thing and tear it to pieces?*

How do you use Internal Monologue and Tone of Voice for maximum impact?

Internal monologue acts at the motivator for the next thing that comes out of the character's mouth. If your character is going to say or do something that the reader might not agree with, give them a good reason to do so by adding in a line of internal monologue. Then, your reader will get behind them, even if they don't agree with them.

Quick Skill - Ask yourself: What is my character thinking right now, and how does it influence what he/she says next?

Then add: What can your character say under thier breath, or even internally, that adds tension to the scene? (Hint—it would be something they wouldn't want the other person in the room to hear!)

Hope this helps as you craft your dialogue!

Conversation #29: The true definition of Showing not Telling

The rain pelleted the parking lot and I glimpsed Sally jumping out of her truck, holding her plastic folder over her head. She dashed into the coffee shop, stood at the door for a moment, shaking off the rain, stamping her feet. She made a face as she shook out her hair and wiped her folder on her jacket then walked over to the counter.

Kathy greeted her, and Sally ordered. She pulled out her smartphone, scrolling down the screen. She frowned, shook her head, then slipped the phone into her pocket.

She went to the condiment table and pried the top off her drink, and the coffee spilled on her hand. She stifled a word, grabbed napkins, and mopped off the table. She added her sugar then closed the top, wadded the napkins into a ball, and threw them into the garbage.

Then she flopped down on the leather chair in the corner opposite me, and sighed.

"Something eating you?"

Her lips made a tight, pinched line on her face, her shoulders rose, fell fast. "I couldn't find my writing bag, and my sitter was late, and I got absolutely no writing done this week…how did you know?"

"Really? Over the next few weeks we're going to talk about one of the most important elements of writing—emotional layering. We'll get to the different layers of emotions next week. But today, I want to lay down a definition for Showing, and not Telling.

"There are a lot of confusing conversations about Showing versus Telling. However, I think many of the conversations center around the wrong topic. Showing is not about describing everything that happens. Showing is about helping the reader experience the emotions and motivations of the character. It's about the reader getting into the character's head to enjoy the journey.

"Let's take a common issue: conveying emotions. If you say: She felt grief, or even (and this is more common), 'Grief overtook her' you are telling us about one emotion you want your reader to feel with the character. It would be better if you showed us how despair makes her feel—physically. Let us into her head.

"Here's an example: She stood at the edge of the closet and stared at his polished shoes, at his pressed wool suits, at his crisp silky red ties. A tidy man. Not the kind to wrap his car around a tree. But there, in the back…she pushed aside the shirts and pulled out his letter jacket, the one he'd wrapped around her the night they'd met. She inhaled. Thirty years, and still his scent lingered. Please, let it linger. Please let her rewind, go back to the fight, erase her words. Erase his anger. Without a word, she stepped inside the closet, closed the door behind her, pulled the jacket over her, and wept.

"Never once do I say that she is grieving—but (hopefully) you get it. The point of showing is to connect us to the POV character more than telling ever could.

"Here's the part that people confuse. Tell actions that are common to all of us. She tied her shoe, she made coffee, she answered the phone. Show actions that you want to make impact. If you want the answering of the phone to have impact, then have her reach for the phone, check the caller ID, maybe hover her thumb over the receive button. Then push it before her courage fails.

"Telling is when you tell someone how to feel. It relates to the emotion in the story. If I had said, 'She stood in front of the closet and grieved,' that would be telling the reader her emotion.

"Further from that, but also a bit like telling, is, 'She stood in front of the closet and felt grief course through her.'

"Better would be, 'She stood in front of the closet and wept.'

"Best would be to use the action—the example I gave."

Sally sighed and closed her eyes.

"Okay, so your homework this week is to simply observe, and maybe write down how people show their emotions. Getting a handle on what emotions look like helps you build your own unique toolkit as a writer."

She had yet to pick up her notebook. "I still don't feel like writing."

I glanced back at Kathy. "I think we're going to need a refill here."

Truth: Showing is about bringing us into the mind and heart of the character to understand their emotional journey.

Dare: Are you bogging down your story by showing actions that have no emotional connection to the story? Ask: How does the emotion impact your character, and how can I show it without telling the reader what the emotion is? Show the reader the emotion, don't tell them that it exists.

Conversation #30: How to Show Emotions—the layers we build into a scene

Dear Sally,

I am sitting in a different coffee shop this morning, in Oregon, missing you, but wanting to continue our conversation about emotional layering.

My flight reminded me of a meeting that occurred a few years ago. I was sitting in the O'Hare Airport when a woman walked into the gate area. She was in her early twenties and carried a backpack, which she held with a whitened fist. She sat down and began to fidget in her seat, checking her watch, looking at the gate, pawing through her bag. She pulled out a book and clutched it to her chest a moment before opening it and taking out a highlighter.

The book's cover said, in large black, ominous letters—*How to Get over Your Fear of Flying*.

Periodically, she wiped her hands on her jeans and blew out a long breath, as if she'd been holding it.

About five minutes before we began to board, she called home. I know, because she spoke into her cell phone loud enough to be heard all the way over in Detroit. "Dad, I'm getting on the flight now. I'll see you soon. Yeah, I'm so nervous, I can barely breathe, but I'll be okay." I could almost hear the pleading voice behind her words saying, "I hope, I hope!"

I said a little prayer for her and got on the plane. I had a window seat.

Of course, she appeared not long afterwards. She had the aisle seat.

I decided to call her Darla. She unpacked her backpack, shoving the *Fear of Flying* book and the highlighter into her seat pocket for easy access, and then shoved her backpack under the seat. She buckled her seat belt, pulling it down tight. She gripped the arm rests and did what I considered early-labor breathing. Sweat dribbled down her brow.

She was starting to freak me out.

Then she looked over at me and said, "I'm a little nervous."

You think?

The short part of the story is that I ended up holding her hand during take-off. This memory reminded me that I wanted to talk to you next about the four layers of character emotions.

See, Sally, a reader doesn't want to be told what to think and feel. They want to discover the story along with the characters—embrace the lessons, experience the pain, and rejoice with the victories. The best stories are the ones that invite the reader into the emotional life of the characters and make a reader invest so much that they can't put the story down.

You do this by bringing your reader into the heart of the character step by step. I call them the four layers of emotions.

The Four Layers of Emotions

1. The first layer of an emotion is simply the surface emotion itself—the name of the emotion. Let's go back to Darla…she turned to me and said, "I'm a little nervous." She stated her emotion.

If I were to write using the first layer of emotions, it would look something like this:

She stood at the entrance to the gateway and fear gripped her. She could not watch the children on the playground without feeling sorrow. Never had she known such happiness as when she saw her son walk off the airplane.

This is a common technique—probably the most common and easy to write. Most people can connect with these feelings and generally can relate to the character. But does it prompt a visceral response? Probably not. Because we're just accessing the information level of the brain. We're agreeing with the emotion, but not necessarily feeling it.

Naming the emotion is a tool to set a tone or to convey a general description of a scene or character. We use this technique a lot for quick emotions, or perhaps as an introductory statement to a paragraph about that emotion. It is not the main emotion of the scene. It does not work to draw your readers into the heart of your character.

So, let's go to the next layer:

2. The second layer is called Just Under the Skin Layer. This layer names the emotion and pairs it with a physical response.

Poor Darla said, "I'm so nervous I can barely breathe." (Yeah, that made everyone feel better.) But through that admission, she connected a little more deeply with us. We often see this layer written in these kind of sentences:

Fear clogged her throat. Dread prickled her skin. Her heart twisted with sorrow.

Fear clogged her throat as she watched the policemen step onto the doorstep. The door locks clicked. Dread prickled her skin.

She watched the woman gather her son into her arms, and her heart twisted with sorrow.

Hopefully we can all understand what it might mean for fear to clog our throats. Putting a physical response to the emotion helps a reader apply their own physical response to the situation. We're now connecting on an informational and physical level. This technique is useful for helping the reader understand the state of mind of the character, putting them in a place of sympathy with the character. The reader can relate, even remember when they have been in a similar place, but it doesn't cause their own physical response.

And we're trying to help them actually feel the emotions with the character.

But, Sally, there's a third layer.

"Sweat dribbled down Darla's brow. She gripped the seats with whitened hands. She practiced early-labor breathing." Even if I hadn't heard her on the phone, I would have gotten it. I don't need to name the emotion to know she's afraid.

3. The next layer is simply the physical response. I call it the Touching the Heart Layer. It's where the reader says, "I have so been there." The reader sees the behavior, or physical action, and the physicality of it reminds them of when they were in the character's exact place.

Here's some phrases an author might use that are simply physical:

Her pulse ratcheted to high. (fear)

Her breath caught. (surprise)

She swallowed hard, her throat parched. (dread)

Her skin prickled at his touch. (creeped out)

Fire streaked through her, right to her toes. (desire)

We're deeper into the character, because we aren't told what emotion to equate with the sense, but rather are left to experience the sense and apply our own experience and emotions to it. We have to dig around inside our heart to decide what emotion that might be, and when we find it, we understand on that heart level what the character is going through. You know I felt sorry for Darla when she began her pre-labor breathing.

This is where a lot of authors stop. They have connected with their readers' hearts, made them feel what their characters feel, and that's their goal.

But there is another layer, one that goes even deeper, one that makes us connect with the character, in an almost spiritual, definitely life-changing connection, and this is the layer I want you to dig for, Sally.

4. This layer is called Soul Deep. It's the use of Action, Metaphor, and other characters to convey emotions. It's the heart of showing.

Darla had a book. A *Fear of Flying* book. She took it out and clutched it to herself, and then almost frantically shoved it back into the bag. Then, after wiping her hands on her pants, breathing out a few times, staring out the window, she grabbed it again, and this time opened it, tearing off the highlighter top with her teeth and going to town, marking up the book, as if it held the key to surviving the next two hours. The book seemed to represent hope and promise and victory, and I saw in my mind's eye a two-year-old clutching his blanket, trembling and alone in the middle of the night in his crib.

I felt sorry for her. If I were to write this metaphor into her POV, it might look like this:

> She didn't need the book. Didn't need…okay, maybe she'd just take it out and hold it. She didn't want it to get lost, maybe left behind. She pressed it to her chest, stared out the window at the airplanes, like birds—safer than cars, the book said—moving around the shiny tarmac. Clear blue skies. A perfect day for flying.
>
> She put the book back in the bag. Shoved it deep. Zipped up the bag. Really, it wasn't like it was a security blanket, or that she was a toddler. Across from her, a woman with a Walkman looked away—Darla knew she'd been staring.
>
> She blew out a breath. Rubbed her greasy palms on her pants. Maybe she should call her father—again. A voice came over the loudspeaker. She tried to listen, but lost the first half of the announcement. What if it was her flight, what if she was left –
>
> She unzipped the pack and wrestled out the book. Opened it. There—"Preboarding: What to Expect at the Gate."
>
> Had she read that chapter? She pulled out the highlighter, held the cap in her mouth and began to underline. Probably she'd just keep the book out.

We never mention that she's afraid. But we see it in her wet palms and breathing—there we touch the heart layer, but most of all we get in her skin through the symbolism and action of needing the book like a security blanket. In the end, the fear wins.

We don't just feel her pain in our hearts. We've been there, wanting to defeat something, and not able to. We've connected with her on a spiritual level, one of deep understanding. Because we understand the metaphor.

Gary Smalley calls it a "word picture"—and tells married couples to use it as they try to communicate. When people can connect to a word picture, they can connect to the emotions we are trying to convey. And when they connect, that's what is going to glue your reader to the page.

For your homework this week, Sally, I want you to look for the four layers of emotions in everything you read and watch. Once you begin to recognize them, it will be easier to understand how to use them.

I can't wait to see you next week!

Warmly,
Susie May

✓**Truth:** Emotional writing is all about drawing your reader into the heart of the character by *showing* them what the emotion looks and feels like, not telling them how to feel.

Dare: Can you identify the four layers of emotion in your own writing? Try writing in the fourth layer, and take the MBT challenge: write a scene without naming the emotion. It's a good exercise—give it a try.

Conversation #31: Techniques for layering emotions: Setting

"I see that you missed me last week. Now, tell me how to write those emotional layers."

I sat down at the coffee shop and Sally was already there, pen in hand, drinking a tall latte.

"You read my letter from last week?"

"I don't appreciate you having coffee without me, but yes," Sally said. Then she winked. "You talked about the different layers of emotions, and drilled down to the last layer, the Soul-Deep layer, or a Word Picture/Symbolic layer. So…how do I write that?" She lifted her pen, poised it over her notebook, and raised an eyebrow.

"There are three ways to work the Soul-Deep layer into a scene:

"Here's is a passage from my current historical, *Baroness*. Note the way I build in the five senses.

The car splashed water onto the sidewalk, dribbling mud onto her dress, her stockings. [touch and sound] She probably looked like a street waif, bedraggled, dirty, starving. Her hair hung in strings around her face and she hadn't stopped to retrieve her coat as she escaped The Valeria. She had however, fled with the pearls, an oversight Cesar wouldn't forget either.

The car turned at the corner, and she stepped out of the alleyway and quick walked down the street. The sun had begun to turn the day dismal and gray, the sky overcast with the pallor of death. (I use a metaphor here, as well a specific sight) Rain spit upon her skin, and a cruel wind licked through her soggy, ruined dress. (Touch) The rain had stirred the dank smells of dirt and rot from the alleyways, (Smell) and she could still taste the tinny rinse of blood in her mouth from where Cesar slapped her. (Taste)

"I'm trying to create a sense of desperation, so I use words like dribbling, dismal, gray, pallor of death, spit, cruel, licked through her, soggy, ruined, dank smells, rot, tinny rinse of blood. Hopefully it helps us understand how she feels. Note that I never name any emotion.

"Why do we get scared when a character walks down the stairs into a creepy basement? We don't even need to know that she's afraid (in fact, sometimes we're more afraid than she is). It's the setting that makes us afraid. This is a way to trick your reader into feeling what your character is feeling by describing the world through their eyes, and inserting meaningful words to convey that emotion.

"Try these hints; pick verbs that convey these emotions: dread, fear, sorrow, joy, peace, hope. Use specific and revealing nouns when describing a scene—the nouns that will convey the most emotions, such as dust, sun, violent music. And find one metaphor that you can use in the scene that captures both the feeling of the scene and the emotion you want to convey.

"Here's what I do—I write the scene. Then I go through and change the verbs to match the mood. I delete any verbs that aren't focused, and any nouns that aren't conveying the emotions in the scene. Then, I look around and find one metaphor from the scene that I can apply to evoke the emotion in the reader.

"Let's take Darla on the plane, a story I used last week. We might use the stuffy, conditioned air—almost a noxious gas—poisoning her as she walks onto the plane. The seat belt, pinning her to the seat, the row upon row of fellow victims, all surrendering their lives into the hands of an unseen deity, not unlike worshippers kneeling before an altar. Then the door closes, forever enclosing them inside, like a tomb.

"I don't know about you, but with those kinds of verbs, nouns and metaphors, I want to run down the aisle screaming, and make them open the door."

Sally laughed. "No more flying for me."

Truth: Setting is a powerful way to build in the Soul-Deep emotional layer for your character by embedding into the setting powerful sensory words that "trick" your reader into feeling what your character feels.

Dare: Can you write the emotion just using your storyworld?

Conversation #32: Techniques for Layering Emotion into a scene: Other People

"Hi Susie. Um, Susie?" Sally sat down in a chair opposite me, handed me a coffee. "Kathy said you forgot this."

I took the cup, tearing my eyes from the woman I'd been watching across the room. She wore a pair of sweatpants, the baggy kind, an oversized sweatshirt, and a bandanna over her hair. Curled up in a leather chair, she was drinking coffee while buried in a novel.

I sighed. "I want to be her. Just take a day off and read."

"That's apparent, by the look on your face," Sally said. "I know you've been busy these past few weeks—hello, I completely feel abandoned, but you look like you want to go rip that book from her hands, push her out of the chair, and take her place."

"I do. Which brings me to our conversation today. We were talking last month about how to layer emotion. I gave some hints about how to use storyworld to trick your reader into feeling the emotion of the scene. Today, we're going to talk about using other people."

"I love to watch people. Especially in an airport. Yes, I admit I compare myself to others—"

"It's a woman thing, I think."

"Right. I've discovered that it's a great way to reveal the emotional landscape of a character. We often project how we feel in how we might describe a character. If I were writing a novel about a stressed woman who sees the casual reader in the corner, I might say it this way:

> Across the room, a woman in sloppy sweatpants, without a care in the world, her hair tied up in a bandanna, sipped a tall cup of coffee. Her nose buried in a book, she appeared oblivious to the chaos, the lines, the patrons barking into their cell phones, the sense of urgency as customers waited for their coffee, checking their watches and their e-mail on their smart-phones. She pulled her knees up, burrowed deeper into the leather chair, and gazed into her novel, a calm, almost peaceful expression on her face. Susie wanted to know what novel could possess the power to pull her away from all the commotion.

"Do you sense a touch of jealousy from the POV character? She almost portrays this woman as irresponsible at first, and then adds in a wistfulness as she wants to know how to have this also.

"You can use this powerful emotional layer technique in two ways.

"First, you can use these other people like a mirror to reflect your character's emotional state."

I glanced at Kathy, at the bar. "If I were to describe Kathy, I might say, 'Kathy raced from the cash register to the frothing machine, barking orders, trying to keep her smile, throwing an occasional glance at the clock. Once, she stared at a customer so long, the woman had to clear her throat and repeat herself. A crazy hush fell over the line, then, people shifting. Susie, wanted to jump the counter, help her fill the orders.'

"So, the woman is harried, and my character feels sorry for her because she knows how it feels to be overwhelmed.

"Another way to use other people is to juxtapose them with the character." I nodded toward the casual reader in the corner. "As I described her, I reflected the description against my own ragged emotions, and my tone became jealous, even wistful, in my description.

"This technique is just a matter of letting your character see someone who embodies the same or opposite emotion as your character, and letting them describe them in their voice, adding inflection, opinion, and using strong verbs and nouns to convey that emotion.

"Try this: look around the scene. Who do you have in the scene who might have been there, done that, in terms of your character's emotions? What do they look like now? Or, is there someone your character would like to emulate? Or even, is there someone your character would never want to be?

"This is another way to 'trick' your reader by layering in the emotions of your character without naming them, but rather bouncing them off an ancillary character. This week, I want you to write another person into the scene who acts as an emotional mirror or opposite to your character's emotions."

But Sally wasn't listening anymore. She too was staring at the woman in the corner. "What book is she reading?"

Truth: You can build in emotions by using other people in a scene to reflect or juxtapose your character's emotions.

Dare: Pick one person in your scene and use them to build the emotional layering of your scene.

Conversation #33: Techniques for layering in emotions: ACTION

"I'm getting the feeling you don't love me anymore." Sally sat down in her chair at the coffee shop.

"I love you. I just love my friends at ACFW and MBT too," I said from the coffee counter. Between school starting and the various writer's conferences over the past two months, we'd barely had time to chat.

"Prove it," she said. "Show me the love."

"I'm here, aren't I?" I was dressed in a football sweatshirt, wearing my Uggs and old jeans. "On my way to a football game. Doesn't that say love?"

She raised an eyebrow.

"Which brings me to the topic of our conversation today—showing emotions through action. And I'm not talking about facial expression or even physical reaction. I'm talking about powerful actions we give our characters to reveal what they feel.

"The last few times we've chatted, we've talked about how to embed emotions into your scenes. We covered the subtle use of storyworld to create a mood, and how to use other people to mirror your characters' emotions. And, before that, we talked about how to show and not tell in regards to emotions.

"However, the strongest way to show emotions is through action. Big actions and small actions can reveal the depth of emotions for your character.

"Here are some examples I've used recently:

"In my book, *You Don't Know Me*, I have Annalise, a woman who is always trying to 'cover up' her past, painting the dark wood paneling in the basement. Later, after a fight, I have Nathan, her husband, go out running, a metaphor for his desire to escape his problems.

"In another scene, Helen, my older heroine, makes apple pie for her friend, Frank, with apples from her tree. Helen wants to build a life with Frank, and her offering of pie is a way to reveal the desires of her heart.

"These 'big actions' provide the framework for the inner desires of my characters and help me set the scene appropriate for their current state of emotions.

"You can also create 'small actions' that reveal your characters' emotions."

I reached into my sweatshirt pocket and pulled out a folded piece of paper. "I brought you a scene. In it, Annalise is feeling stuck, and emotionally raw and helpless. So I put her in the kitchen, creating these feelings in the words and actions of scrubbing the Sunday afternoon football dishes."

"Oh good, read-aloud time," Sally said.

"Annalise dumped the gnawed chicken wings into the trash then set the tray in the sink. She squirted dishwashing liquid onto it, turned the hot water on full blast. The barbecue sauce from the wings needed soaking to work free.

Behind her in the next room, opposite the kitchen, her family cheered on the Sunday night game. The Eagles were down against *the Patriot*s by one touchdown late in the third quarter.

Based on the roar of her crowd, the Eagles had just managed a fantastic run. Or catch. Or something. Not that she cared oh-so-much about football, but Nathan loved it, so she did too.

Or pretended to.

Her life had become one big game of pretend.

At least it suddenly seemed like it. Three days ago, it felt real and right and whole. Three days ago she was Annalise Decker. Today she felt like Deidre O'Reilly.

And today she wanted to call her mother. To hear her voice, to tell her how sorry she was, every day, over and over.

She picked up a scrubber and began to attack the pot, not caring how the hot water scalded her."

"Sad," Sally said.

"Here's another one. In this one, Annalise longs to turn back time, keep Colleen young, and repair their broken relationship. So, she climbs into bed with her teenage daughter, just like she might have when she was six, and holds onto her."

"Now I'm feeling all guilty about being so demanding."

"You should.

"Colleen had closed her door, and Annalise listened a moment before she turned the handle and eased it open. Colleen lay on her side, curled into her covers. Annalise couldn't stop herself. She tiptoed into the room and climbed onto the bed, molding herself to her daughter's frame, tucked under the covers.

Her daughter breathed the rhythmic melody of slumber. Annalise draped her arm over Colleen's body, settling it lightly. Colleen didn't stir. Then Annalise closed her eyes and breathed in the sweet smell of her baby's skin as she listened to the words of their fight."

"Makes me want to go home and hug my kids."

"Good." I put the pages away. "Consider both the big-picture scenes, and the smaller actions that can contribute to revealing the emotions of your character. Remember, 'show don't tell' is directly related to emotion—so use your storyworld, other characters, and powerful actions to help us feel the emotions of your characters.

"Here's your latte," Kathy, our barista said, and handed me a spiced chai pumpkin latte.

I handed it to Sally. "These are your favorite, right?"

She laughed. "Okay, you win. I feel the love!"

Truth: Revealing emotions in your character is a subtle, complex equation of the right scene, the right setting, the right actions, and the right characters.

Dare: Write the emotions using simply Action. Better—act it out for a friend or reader. Do they know how you feel?

Quick Skills: 5 Common Mistakes and how to fix them

Not starting the story with a compelling situation. So many rough drafts start in a place where the author is either explaining the character's backstory or creating the storyworld instead of getting to the character and creating a situation where we see him interacting with his world, setting up for the Inciting Incident (or even in the middle or after it).

Remember, the first three chapters of your novel are the "drive" chapters, the chapters that propel your reader into the story. You need powerful language and scenes to hook your reader. Most of all, there must be something at *stake* that makes the reader care and want to read more.

Quick Skills Fix—Ask: What does my character have to lose in this scene/chapter/book? What will happen if they don't accomplish their goal?

Your character must have something to lose, or we won't care if he wins the day or not. This is why people don't watch preseason football, or the Probowl. There is nothing at stake. Insert this risk/fear of losing into your scene/chapter/book, and you will have created a compelling element to your story.

Short scenes. At the beginning of a book, it is essential to build that storyworld, characterization, and stakes, and it's nearly impossible to do this with a short scene. We need to get into the story, wade around, see the parts, and get deep enough to be taken by the current. Aim for at least twelve hundred words.

Quick Skills Fix—Ask: Is my Scene an Action scene or a Reaction scene? After determining what kind of scene it is, make sure you have all three components built into your scene:

Action = Goal + Conflict + Disaster (or new problem)

Reaction = Reaction + Dilemma + Decision (or new goal)

After you have established these three goals, then make sure you have added:

Storyworld—including the five senses!

Dialogue—Are you putting the story between the quotes?

Conflict—is there enough conflict?

Not ending the chapter in a place that makes the reader want to read more. So many scenes are ending with the tension resolved. If you do this, the reader doesn't want to read more! Keep the tension going, or introduce new tension and your reader will go onto chapter two!

Quick Skills Fix—Ask: What unexpected yet plausible situation could happen at the end of this scene that would whet the reader's interest?

What does your character fear the most, right now? Could you make that happen?

Not having a complete character journey. This means an inner as well as an outer journey (remember, the outer journey is just the catalyst for the inner journey) as well as an Inciting Incident, Black Moment Event, and Epiphany. Your story has no point without these elements. Also, be aware of creating realistic motivation. The motivations for your character's actions must make sense.

Quick Skills Fix: Create a "Push-Pull" for every scene. Every scene has to have an emotional or physical Push/Pull (or combination thereof). It's the Push away from something negative, and the Pull toward something positive.

Tired writing. Clichés, passive writing, mundane dialogue, and most of all, bad writing. Like mixed metaphors (when in doubt, don't use a metaphor!), and terrible emotional content. "His heart banged inside him like a parade of marching band cadets" is *not* good emotional writing. Neither is, "Panic bombarded her like an avalanche of snow." Don't give us expected, soap opera emotions—go deeper and really ask how to create an emotion that feels real. Please, think through how this emotion really feels, and show it through your character's actions, dialogue, inner thoughts, and even the setting.

Quick Skills Fix—Ask: What is your character feeling right now (as the scene opens)? When have you felt this way? How did you act/feel? What did you say? Pull from your experiences to create realistic emotions.

Quick Skills: These common mistakes are easily avoided if you take the time to look for them. And you'll be surprise at how they strengthen your story!

3½

Conversation #34: From Good to Great—Revisiting the Importance of Tension.

I could see Sally's breath crystallize in the air as she jogged up to the coffee shop door. Bruised and soggy leaves layered the parking lot—red, gold, purple. The sun had just baked the frost from the pink chrysthanthemums blooming outside.

Our little town crouched at the edge of winter—we could feel it in the air. The crisp tension of autumn, when any day we'd wake to a snowfall.

The door jangled as Sally opened it. She caught my eye. "Sorry I'm late." She dropped her backpack onto her chair. "Field trip day at school and I forgot to sign a permission slip. Congratulations on the game Friday night. I heard your son ran for a touchdown, and the other made a sack. I'll bet it was fun to watch."

"I wish. I was on an airplane, heading home, listening to our hometown radio on the in-flight Internet. I would hear the beginning of the play and then the connection would time out and I'd struggle to get it back. I missed about half of it fighting with the Internet and holding my breath."

"How stressful."

"Exactly." I couldn't help note the frown on Sally's face. "What?"

"You know what's stressful? Writing a boring book!" Her hand rested on a stack of printed manuscript papers. "I mean, the story is good…in my head. But it seems to lack…well, let's put it this way; my husband fell asleep somewhere between pages 87 and 103."

"Oh my," I said, sipping the latte. Just the right balance of whipped crème sweetness and pumpkin pie spice. "So, what do you think is the problem?"

"He says I have a great story, with great storyworld and fun dialogue and even good emotional layering. It's just…well, he says the scenes are boring."

"This can be fixed, Sally, don't despair. What you have is the right ingredients for the second layer of a scene: Storyworld, Emotional layering, dialogue, and even metaphors. However, none of these matter if you haven't built the first layer, or the foundation: the scene tension."

"Wait—didn't we talk about that six months ago? You want me to remember that now?"

"Okay, now that you've learned how to put a book together, create storyworld and emotions, and are writing your scenes, it's the perfect time to review how to create tension in those scenes.

"Remember, tension is what drives every scene, and is created by a combination of elements all doing their part, much like a sports team. It's a combination of a Sympathetic Character + Stakes + Goals + Obstacles + Fear of Failure. If any of these are missing, you don't have tension, and are simply muddling along.

"Without a Sympathetic Character, we don't care about what happens to him. Without something to lose (Stakes), it doesn't matter whether he wins or not. Without a reason to be there (Goals) he could just go home. Without something to push against (Obstacles), there is no conflict. Most importantly, without the real Fear of Failure, we don't care. If we know they will accomplish their task, then why even bother to show us the scene?

"The Scene Tension Equation is why we love football or sporting events. We have our team (Sympathetic Character), we have the game and our record to defend (Stakes), the Goal is to win, the Obstacle is the other team, and of course if they are not good, if they are not fighting back just as hard, then it's not a great game. We love games where we win by the skin of our teeth, don't we? A hard-fought battle? We have to believe we could lose in order for the game to take on resonance.

"Let's go back to me on the plane. I'm the sympathetic character: a dedicated mom trying to balance career and family. I haven't missed a game yet this year, and it's my son's senior year. These are the personal stakes. I might even raise the stakes by making it a playoff game and potentially his last game of the season. The goal is to cheer him on and let him know I am supporting him (in other words, he'll ask if I caught his game). The obstacles are the travelling and the spotty nature of the in-flight Internet. And when the connection times out twice before the game starts, there's a real fear of failure."

Sally was taking notes. "I get it. I was the sympathetic heroine this morning trying to get my kids ready for school. My goal was to get my son to school on time for the field trip. The obstacles were my son's missing backpack and the fact we overslept. The stakes were that this field trip counted for part of his grade. And the fear of failure was the reality that he'd missed the last field trip."

"Sounds like a doozy of a morning." I glanced at Kathy, who was already fixing Sally a pumpkin chai. "Sally, your homework this week is to go through every scene and ask: Why should I care about this character and this scene? What's at stake? What are the Goals and Obstacles, and finally, do I fear the character might fail? Answering these questions for every single scene will help you reshape your story into something that won't put your husband to sleep."

Sally closed her book. Accepted the chai from Kathy with a smile. "Can I just sit here for a moment first, and breathe?"

Truth: Wordsmithing can only get you so far in a story; if you don't have tension, your book will suffer the "put it down in the middle" syndrome. To keep the tension high in the story, you need to carefully craft the tension equation into each scene. You might feel these elements by instinct, but getting deliberate with your tension elements will help you craft a novel that your readers can't put down.

Dare: For every scene, do a quick litmus test: Do you have the Scene Tension elements? Analyze every scene and build in the right foundation before you add in the riveting details.

Conversation #35: How to Write a Book in a Month

"Don't ask me to write a novel in a month. I'm sorry, it's just too overwhelming."

Sally took a sip of her mint dark chocolate cocoa, looking at me as if I'd asked her to run a marathon. Tomorrow. "No. Forget it."

"You're about halfway in, right? And overwhelmed? And you've learned so much. What about setting this book aside and simply jumping in with a new one with all you've learned? Or maybe, just committing to finishing this one. Technically, NaNoWriMo (National Novel Writing Month) is about finishing a new story, but that doesn't mean you can't take the principles and apply it to a current story and finish it."

"Fifty-five thousand words in a month…?" She took another, very long sip of cocoa.

"Listen, Sally. You can do this. Plan the work, then work the plan –"

"That's easy for you to say–you've done that about forty times!"

"And I do it the same way each time." I pulled out a sheet of paper. "I made you this cool infographic of the process. Just follow it step by step." Found Here: http://learnhowtowriteanovel.com/wp-content/uploads/2014/10/MBT-WriMo-Infographic-MASTER.jpg

She took the graphic. "I'm going to need more than this, Coach, to get me through to the end."

"Fine. Next week I'll bring a Scene starter. In the meantime…what do you want to write about?"

"I think I'd like to just finish the current book I'm on."

"Super. Let me give you a few pointers on how to get the story on paper.

"First, I'm assuming you've done all your prework—your characterization, plotting, and most importantly, told yourself the story. This synopsis, despite how long and rough it is, will be your roadmap. You simply need to sit down each day and see where you are. Yes, you'll probably veer away a little, but as long as you keep your destination in mind, you won't spend hours later rewriting."

"You're really persistent about that whole, 'tell yourself the story' thing."

"Well, it pays to see if you have a story to tell, and whether you like it or not before you commit to writing it. And, you have a deadline—one month. So you don't have the luxury of wandering around, waiting for the story to discover you. So, yeah."

"Which is how you write three to four novels a year."

"It's one of my tricks, yes. But I learned it from other career novelists—and frankly, you'll need to learn how to write a synopsis in order to sell a book on proposal (before you write it), so it's a great skill to learn."

"Fine."

"Then, once you have your map, set a specific time every day to write. You'll do your writing at this time—and all the scene development in the in-between time. That way you'll maximize your time. Your scene development is your character interview, your Scene Creation checklist and even mulling over the first line. You can do this while you're driving kids to school, exercising—"

"Ha!"

"Or even lying in bed, just relaxing. Sometimes I just sit in a chair and think. But all of that is the pre-work to writing. If it helps, call a friend and talk through the scene you're going to create, just so you get the structure, tension, and emotions right.

"Then, when you sit down to write, set yourself a word count and push through. Don't look at Facebook, Twitter, your e-mail, or even answer your phone. I have a sign on my door that says, "*Cry Me A River*," and unless there is blood or smoke, kids have to enter quietly and wait for me to talk to them."

"Seriously? What, are your kids heavily sedated?"

I laughed.

"What do I do once I reach my word count for the day? Go back and read it?"

"No. If you do that, you'll get bogged down with rewriting. Just keep going. Keep telling the story. One thing that helps is to keep a revisions list of all the things you want to change/add during your next session. This allows your brain to stay calm, knowing you'll go back and change it later. One thing that helps your momentum is to note your total word count as you go—it gives you that boost to keep going. I'll give you some pointers on what to do after you've finished."

"You have more confidence than I do."

"I know you, Sally. Your homework is…keep writing!"

Truth: Writing a book in a month is about the pre-work, the scheduled writing time, and pushing for a goal. It's not for everyone, but it can be a jumpstart to finishing a novel, or starting one you've been dreaming of writing.

Dare: You don't have to join NaNoWriMo to write a book in a month. Set a deadline for yourself and push hard to finish. Your sense of accomplishment each day will motivate you to the next!

Conversation #35: NaNoWriMo Encouragement

"How is your NaNoWriMo manuscript going?" I set my coffee down at the table where Sally sat waiting for me, drinking coffee and eating a cookie. A light frost tipped the grass outside, the lake frothy along the rocky shoreline.

"I think my brain is shutting down. I've written about two thousand words a day, but I'm running out of ideas to create fresh, interesting scenes." Sally broke off a piece of her monster cookie, the fresh-baked smell enough to make me wish I hadn't eaten breakfast.

"Have you done your scene preparation? Figured out Layer One— what kind of scene it is, and the 5 Ws'?"

"Oh, that's the easy part. And Layer Two isn't so hard either. Creating Tension is easy once you understand the equation: a Character we care about who has a goal, as well as something to lose, who meets obstacles that feel so insurmountable that we fear they'll fail."

"Right. The equation is: Sympathetic Character + Stakes + Goals + Obstacles + Fear of Failure."

"I have a lot of Fear of Failure right now." She broke off another piece of cookie. An M&M dropped onto her napkin. "It just feels like I'm writing the same old stuff...everyone is smiling and shrugging and there's nothing original. And... all the preparation feels too contrived. I'd like to let the scene just...flow out of me.

Organic. Seat of the pants. Except, yes, I'm a bit stumped as to how to make it exciting."

I looked at her cookie as she finished it off. "When you make cookies, you use the same ingredients for almost every kind of cookie. Sugar. Flour. Eggs. Salt. Baking soda. Have you ever started making cookies and realized you've run out of one of the ingredients? Suddenly you have to run to the store, and your baking is stalled.

"The same thing happens when you're creating a scene. First, you assemble your ingredients. If you skip this part, you don't know what you're missing, and you'll suddenly be stalled in your creation process.

- "When you do your writing pre-work, you're pulling your scene 'ingredients' out of the cupboard (your head) before you start mixing it together. You're still writing the scene 'Seat of the Pants' but you're using specific ingredients to help you build it. And since you've assembled them beforehand, you can write without having to stop and figure out what you're missing. Your homework is simply to stop before every scene and do your prework—it'll be worth it."

"I see you eyeing my cookie."

"I did mention the other secret to getting words on the page, right? Chocolate."

Truth: Success in scene building and maximizing your writing session is about preparation and gathering your ingredients before you begin.

Dare: Do your prep work before you begin your writing session. A few minutes of planning will save you an hour of staring at an empty page!

Conversation #36: Understanding (and plotting) Turning Points

"I'm so sorry," Sally said, sitting down and unwrapping her scarf from her neck. Outside, ice glazed the puddles, the sky a slate gray. The first hint of snow hung in the air, the world of northern Minnesota in crisp expectation.

I love the change of seasons. I blew on my candy-cane mint mocha. "Why?"

"Our high school football season is over," she said. "I know how you love to go to the games."

I do. I live for the Friday night lights. "It was a tough game. A number of game-changing moments that could have turned the game our way. Our boys fought a tough fight."

"I heard that on the second play of the game, the other team got past our defense and ran for a touchdown."

"Yes, and then when we got the ball, we fumbled, and they ran it back for another touchdown. Two touchdowns in less than five minutes of play."

"Pretty tough for an undefeated team."

"Yes. Suddenly, the game became a fight. Can you say Noble Quest?"

She smiled. "Is everything about writing with you?"

"Yes. I've often said that a football game is like a novel—the teams are the protagonist and antagonist and the downs represent scenes. I like this analogy because it also works for understanding the difference between Turning Points and Bumps in the Road. Which is what I want to talk to you about today.

"I know that you are fast-drafting, and you might think we should have talked about this much earlier, but sometimes it can be challenging to see your Turning Points before you've put down a rough draft. With so much going on in the Second Act of your novel, how do you distinguish the real Turning Points from the other steps along the journey?"

"I'll be honest—I haven't given one thought to Turning Points," Sally said. "But I know I have to have them…right? What are they?"

"Okay, hang with me, because I'm going to talk about football again.

"After the two touchdowns by the other team, our players realized they had to do something different if they wanted to win. We entered into Act 2 of our game/story/noble quest.

- "In order to win, we had to change how we played defense and stop the other team from running the ball. Our strategy worked, and the other team was forced to start passing the ball. Which is what we wanted…until they completed a pass and ran it in for yet another touchdown."

"Bummer."

"Or, we might call that a teaching moment or Turning Point. Because our players had to figure out what to do. They needed to score, so they rearranged their offense and drove down the field for a touchdown."

"Yay!"

"That was another Turning point, and the mood of the game

changed. We came out at the second half with a new defensive and offensive strategy…and it worked."

"Sadly, it wasn't enough to win."

"Thank you, Sally. But, we learned from the mistakes of the first quarter, and by the time we finished the game, we not only played our best, but we felt triumphant about how we'd grown as a team. We had nothing to be ashamed of, despite our loss."

"I agree," Sally said. "Great season."

"All right, enough about football. Let's apply this to our Act 2.

"Act Two of your novel is the part where your character confronts his Flaws and fears and begins the process of character change. Act Two is fraught with obstacles, challenges, decisions, and frustrations that require your character to learn new things about himself, all of which culminates in the Epiphany of Act 3 and then causes him to finish his journey victoriously.

"Turning Points in a novel are those big plays that change the course of a story. They add new stakes, new trouble, even victories. The purpose of a Turning Point is to teach your character something they'll need in order to achieve victory.

"People often define a Turning Point as a crisis —and yes, this can be a turning point. But think back to your own life. Sometimes it isn't a crisis that turns us from our course, but some sort of event, decision, information, or even obstacle on our journey. We need to start thinking of Turning Points as those things that teach us something. They open the door to new lessons, opportunities, and relationships.

"If you are writing your scenes correctly, you'll have a goal, an obstacle, and stakes for every scene. Often, these will also have a crisis of some kind. But not every scene can act as a turning point. It would simply be too high drama. Imagine a football player fumbling or scoring in every play."

"I thought we were done talking about football."

"Right. Okay, bumps in the road are the smaller roadblocks or mini-problems that occur during the Turning Point sections. They may be a result of the Turning Point, or contribute to the turning point. They may reinforce a lesson or a fear. But most of all, they simply contribute to the impact of the turning point.

"Bumps in the road in a football game might be a quarterback getting sacked. Or a badly thrown pass.

"Turning Points in a football game are touchdowns or turnovers. That's when the other team gets the ball—"

"Susie –"

"Stay with me. Turning Points are the big events in a story that require us to learn and adjust and then keep going."

"Ah."

"Right. So, your homework is, as you're writing this week to look at your novel and ask, do you have two to three turning points in your novel, with bumps in the road between each one?"

Outside, flakes began falling past the window.

"Here's to next season," Sally said, holding up her mug.

"Here's to basketball," I said with a wink.

Truth: A great story has two to three big turning points in Act 2 that drive the character forward and teaches him a mini-lesson (or confirms a mini-lie) that will be used in the Climax/Black Moment Event and Epiphany.

Dare: Watch a movie this week and see if you can find the Act 2 Turning Points. Can you find the Turning Points in your own novel?

Conversation #37: The Difference between a Rough Draft and the Final Draft

I found Sally in line as I entered the coffee shop. She had already dumped her bag onto a chair, had already tugged off her gloves and her wool jacket, and wore her game face.

"What's up?"

"I'm 3,000 words away from finishing my novel."

"That's great." I shed my jacket and motioned to Kathy. She gave me a smile, already on my order.

"No so much." She retrieved her coffee and handed me mine. I nodded my appreciation.

"Why?"

"Because I only have 46,000 words and I'm near the end of my novel."

"And?"

"It' supposed to be an 80,000 word novel! How am I going to come up with 30,000 more words?"

"Oh, I see. You think just because you finished NaNoWriMo with a 50,000 word manuscript, that you're done. Mmmhmm."

"Well, I know it needs editing...."

"Sally. What you have created is the shell of your novel. You've put down every great scene you can think of, and because you are racing through the novel to write it—because that is the point of NaNoWriMo—you are hitting all the big events. I bet you have sentences like, 'She argued with him until she got her way,' and 'They talked over dinner and she decided that she liked him.' Or even, 'She got into the car at 7am, late for work and angry.'"

"So? What's your point?"

"Take a breath. This is normal. You've rushed into your story and through your scenes so you can quickly download the story from your head to the page without losing it. That's excellent. Now that you have the framework of your story, you have to go back and add the furniture, the decorative touches. Storyworld and description and emotional layering.

"Let's return to those simple sentences. Instead of telling us that the argument happened, how about letting us hear that argument? We want to be a part of it.

"Instead of telling us about their date, how about really putting us in the scene, letting us hear the dialogue?

"Or, how about showing us what it feels like to get in the car at 7am, late and angry in the middle of a Minnesota winter?

"The sunrise simmered over the far horizon, hot lava spilling over the tops of the birch and pine trees, splashing down upon the frost that covered her windshield. She opened the car door with a creak and fished around for the scraper. Shoot, she'd left it in the other car. Digging through her purse, she found her old fitness club card. Well, it wasn't like she'd use that anytime soon. She attacked the front windshield, drawing thick lines through the frost, the ice curling up over her bare fingers, turning them numb.

Maybe the rest of her could turn numb, too—anything to stop the roaring heat inside that was sure to spill over onto Malcolm the minute she walked into the office.

How could he steal her presentation?

"Okay, so I made up Malcolm—"

"I already hate him."

"But see, instead of telling us how she felt, I drew you into the scene slowly, letting the reader really see it. Your WriMo scenes are essential, because they've provided the framework of your story. You now need to go back and flesh out each scene, adding in all the beautiful details, the storyworld, the characterization, the dialogue, the emotions, and the metaphors. You've only just begun. You can sing along if you'd like."

Sally was smiling now.

"Feel better?"

"Yes. It's like I finally get to read the story I've written."

"Exactly. You've done the hard work of building the house. Now this is the fun part—decorating."

"Just in time for Christmas."

Truth: The first draft of your story just builds the story foundation. Even if you are a "pantster" you'll need to go back and add in the rich details and layers to make your story satisfying.

Dare: Finish your fast-draft, then go back and allow yourself time to rebuild, decorate, and savor the story you've written.

Conversation #38: Macro-Editing your Fast Draft

"Okay, here it is." Sally plunked down a thick sheaf of paper, bound by a rubber band. "72,834 words."

"I'm impressed." I handed her a victory candy-cane mocha.

"I'm exhausted. My brain is a noodle. I wrote late at night, early in the morning, while boiling macaroni and cheese. I've thought about this novel in my sleep, while doing laundry, driving my kids to school. All I do is think about this book."

"But do you like it?"

She glowed. "I do. But it needs so much work, and I'm not sure where to start. I have a jumbled mess. I have misspelled words and run-on sentences and grammatically incorrect paragraphs...ugly."

"No worries. Today, I'm going to tell you what to do with that mess!

"First, Let your Brain Rest. Set the story aside. Hopefully, you took notes during the creation phase. For at least a day—maybe even three—set your story aside and let it marinate. You'll be thinking of all the things you might want to add, different layers and themes, etc. Keep a notebook of these ideas.

"Do other things. Exercise, clean the house, cook, go for walks. Let your brain breathe. Read another book. Seriously. You'll be reminded of layers to add or scenes you might want to put in."

"That sounds perfect," Sally said. "I have a stack of books I want to read. And I should probably clean my house."

"But you're not quite done yet. After you've rested, then it's time for the Storycrafter Overhaul."

"I start with the Quick and Dirty Touch up: I gather up my notes and implement them. I like to do this right away, before I forget them. But I'm still in the rough-draft stage."

"If I have big rewrites, then I wait until the next step to implement them. This step is about adding in metaphors and names, and food and clothing. But, if I have to add big scenes, then I put those in the Macro-Edit Stage."

Overhaul: Now start to look at the big pieces. We're talking Macro-Story Edits. I go through my entire book and check the structure. Do I have the big pieces?

Dark Moment—Greatest Fear/Lie

Happy Moment—Heal the Wound, happy ending?

LINDY HOP—Do I have the structure?

Final Battle ending?

Then, I look for my Essential Scenes—the Scenes I must have in every novel:

I usually have the big ones, but I often forget a couple:

Meet the Hero, or Heroine

If I could only—What stands in my character's way of storming the castle and rescuing the princess?

All I want is to be Happy—the story about his fondest memory and why, and what his greatest dream is.

Why I'll never love again—the revelation of his past romances. We need to know what holds him back.

Out of Character scene—have him do something that goes contrary to his goals.

What if I lose everything scene—This shows us what is at *stake* as well as what he fears.

Black Moment event scene…You can't have a book without this scene! This is what causes him to change!

- Breakdown/Epiphany Scene. This is his change, the truth that sets him free!

The Sacrificial Act. It makes him heroic, but also changes him into the person he needs to be. (What can he do at the end that he couldn't do at the beginning? Show the reader that he is a new, improved person!)

- After I have overhauled the Story and have all the Structure in place, that's when I start on the Scene-by-Scene editing."

"Stop! That's enough for this week." Sally pressed her hands to her head.

"Breathe, Sally. Drink your cocoa. Watch the snowflakes. Read a good book. You deserve it."

Truth: Every Fast Draft needs editing. The first draft is just the raw material—you will need to analyze and rewrite.

Dare: Take a breath, take a day or two, even a week to let your brain rest, then go through the macro edits of your story and make sure you have the big pieces before you start the scene-by-scene edits!

Conversation #39: Scene-by-Scene Editing

"So much snow!" Sally came into the coffee shop stamping her feet. Overnight, the sky had buried our little village in thick frosting.

I sat nursing a hot cocoa. "I know. It feels a little overwhelming, thinking of plowing the driveway, the porch, and the deck."

"Not unlike doing the macro edit on my novel," Sally said, unwinding her scarf. "But I think I have the big picture/content edits figured out. What's next?"

Kathy handed her a peppermint mocha. Sally sat down, warming her hands on the cup.

"Now it's about looking at every scene to make sure it has enough tension and that you're building in the emotional layers. I call it Scene-by-Scene Editing.

"First, start with the scene structure. Determine if it is an Action or ReAction scene. Then define your goals, conflict, disaster, or your response, dilemma, decision.

"Then, use the Scene Tension equation and make sure you have built enough story tension!"

"So, look at the Scene Structure first. Done," Sally said.

"Yes. After your Scene Structure is in place, then it's time to see if

2) you delivered through the Scene Elements. In other words, have you drawn the reader into the world of the Character? Here are the editing questions to ask yourself:

- Have I built in enough Storyworld?

- Do I have the Who, What, When, Where and Why?

- Do I have the five senses?

- Have I created a mood with the use of my five senses and the verbs and nouns I use?

- Have I used the right POV?

- Would the scene have more impact if it was in a different POV?

- Do I have enough Dialogue in the scene?

- "Dialogue moves a story and creates tension. If you have even one page without Dialogue, insert something—a remembered conversation, a phone conversation, even a letter or journal entry to create another voice.

  "Have you created sparks with your dialogue? If it feels tired and expected, have your character say something they shouldn't—that should cause some tension!

- Have I created Emotion through Action?

  "Give your character something to do, and have his action convey his emotions. What does the character do because of the way he/she feels?

  "And here's the biggest question: Have I glossed over important moments in my rush to get to the end of the scene? Have I allowed my reader to experience every important nuance of the scene?

  "Slow it down. Describe the scene. Take your time. Your character will still go off the cliff—you are just helping the reader understand how dangerous it is and how hard he tries to stop it.

  "And, speaking of cliffs—don't forget to end each scene with a new problem!

"The mark of a great novelist is their ability to draw you into the world they see and allow you to feel it with the character."

"It's only after I do this phase that I begin to start wordsmithing—really fine-tuning the words."

Sally gaped at me. "Seriously? There's another editing phase after this?"

"Two more, in fact. But just do this for now, or you'll get overwhelmed. Or"—I took a sip of my cocoa—"some might say… snowed in."

"Ha," she said.

Truth: Editing a story is best accomplished by looking at the big picture first, then the individual scene. Does your story deliver the emotional impact?

Dare: Look at your scene structure before you dive into the scene, and you'll have a better understanding of how to weave in the scene elements.

Conversations #40: Wordsmithing your story to perfection

Sally sat down at the table, handing me a Christmas tin. "Merry Christmas."

I opened it. Inside lay petite gingerbread men and women, their faces, aprons, and overalls intricately decorated. "Wow."

"It's my one Christmas claim to fame. I sell them at the annual craft show."

They looked too good to eat. "You put me to shame. My talents end with chocolate chip cookies. Although, my children love them."

I put the lid on the tin. "You know, your cookie prowess is not unlike finding your Voice, or wordsmithing your story. Which is the final step in editing your manuscript before you move to proofing."

"I am nearly finished with all my scene-by-scene edits."

"Then you're ready to make your story sing. It's in the wordsmithing phase where an author's Voice really emerges…in the delivery of the story on the page."

"First, you have to start with the Mechanics. Go through your grammar and hone your writing. Here's a checklist:

1. Are there five senses in each scene?

2. Replace the adverbs with strong verbs, the adjectives with defined nouns. Cut as many "ly" ending adverbs as possible.

3. Be ruthless with passive sentences. "Was" and "were" are good clues to a passive sentence. Although sometimes you need a passive sentence to let the reader rest, most of your sentences should be active.

4. Repeating sentences—If two sentences say virtually the same thing, cut one.

5. Two adjectives together weaken both. Use the strongest one.

6. Read through your dialogue—Do you need tags? Do you have enough action between words? Do you repeat names? Do you need to delete tags to make it faster? Is there enough white space between chunks of dialogue? Body language? Fighting words?

7. Do you have a list of overused words? Do a word search and fix/delete those!

• "Now comes the fun part. Turn your page landscape view, click 'select all,' and make two columns. Change to single space. It will look like a printed book! I like to change the typestyle to Garamond or Bookman to really get the feel of reading a novel.

"Take two days and simply read your story, feeling the words, how they convey the emotions, how they lay on the page. Look for overwriting—have you repeated words, sentences, paragraphs, concepts?

• Using a red pen, take your time and edit a hard copy. Change words around, add new sentences...you are reading the book for the emotional effect it has on the reader.

In the back of your mind, do a final story check and ask deeper question, the ones that create an impact on your reader:

• Scenes—Do your scenes pack a punch? Do each of your scenes have a purpose? Do you need to make the slower scenes faster? Can you combine two slow scenes, cutting away the less important for the more important?

Action—Are there sufficient reasons for everything your character does in that scene? Have you planted the clues for that action or decision long before they do it?

Likeable characters—Does your hero/heroine have great qualities that make you truly like them? Make sure that in each scene, there is something likeable about your character—that special spark that sets them apart.

Then I look at the art. Do the sentences sing to you? Can your characters be a bit more creative in their dialogue? Have you used your nouns and verbs in a powerful way? Have you woven in symbolism? Do you like it?

Then, I fix it, proof it…pray over it, and it's ready for readers!"

"Whalla!" Sally shook her head.

"You're almost done. Remember—the difference between rearranging words and editing is that editing adds emotion, texture, precision, and mood to a scene. Always ask: How has my wordsmithing made my scene more powerful?"

"I can't believe I've almost finished a book in a year."

"Sally, I'm so proud of you. I can't wait to read your story. Next week, I'll give you some hints on how to sell it."

"Next week is Christmas Eve. You're not going to make me work on Christmas Eve are you?"

I opened the tin and took out a gingerbread man. I smiled and bit off his head.

Truth: A final manuscript takes many readings, each for a different purpose. Don't rush through it or you'll miss the nuances that make a story powerful.

Dare: Go through your story yet again and work on the storytelling—the wordsmithing and story impact questions. If you've crafted the right structure, then these are the elements that will stand out to your reader and create a story that they want to pass along.

The Last Conversation: The Next Chapter

"I like your jacket," I said as Sally sat down at the table. She un-Wound a knitted scarf, rich with reds and greens.

"Christmas gifts, as well as these." Sally held out fingerless gloves. "For typing on cold days."

"Perfect. How is the editing going?"

"I'm finished, or at least, for now. I sent the latest and greatest to a group of friends to read, and I'm looking at a conference to attend so I can pitch it to an editor."

"I'm proud of you, Sally. You've learned so much this year—"

"I know. I have this strange euphoria. Ideas follow me into the night and I can't wait to get started on my next story."

"It's because you realized…you can write a book. All the way to the end. Nothing feels better than finishing something. And finishing a novel is huge. So…what are the big lessons about writing a novel you would tell others hoping to pursue their dreams?"

Sally ran her finger around the rim of her coffee cup.

"First, that writing a story is both harder and easier than I thought. It's daunting, yes, but taken apart step by step, and with patience, it can be done. However, it's a lot more intricate than I imagined. It's both an art and a science, I guess.

"Then, I'd say a great story takes a lot of thought and polish. You have to really think through what you want to say, and why you are writing. And you have to keep that focus all the way to the end of the story."

I nodded.

"I think I'd also suggest getting a coach, or someone who understands your story and can ask you the right questions. Even if it isn't a fellow writer, it could be someone who is willing to listen to you ramble.

"And I'd also suggest getting some of my writing books—like *The Story Equation*, and *The Brilliant Book Buddy*—to help."

"I'm in agreement with that," I said.

She grinned.

"And finally, I'd say—you never know what you can do if don't try. Writing a book has caused me to discover things about myself, and to push myself to new emotional places, and to figure out what I really want in life. It's made me a better person, I think, and given me something I can leave behind."

"So, it was worth the journey?" I asked.

She lifted a bound manuscript from her bag. "Yes."

"What's this?"

"*What if I Loved You*, my novella. It's just the rough draft, but I hope you like it."

[You can get that novella here: http://learnhowtowriteanovel.com/wp-content/uploads/2016/09/What-If-I-Loved-You.pdf

I gave her a hug. "I believe you just might be my next favorite author. Thanks for letting me coach you this year. It's been my pleasure."

"Thanks, Coach. Mine too."

Note: I hope you enjoy Sally's book. Not bad for a first-timer! Thank you to Sarah May Erredge for allowing me to use her story, her questions, and her writing journey in this book.

Personal Words from your Coach:

I am absolutely inspired by the Olympic Athletes, their dedication to their sport, the sacrifices they make, the drive inside, their ability to envision victory that propels them forward.

I love both the team and the individual events. Like rowing! And the synchronized diving? Amazing. My favorite, however, is swimming. For a brief time, I swam competitively (I wasn't very good), and watching the events brings back the feeling of adrenaline, the competitive burn, the sense of cutting through the cool water.

It brings me back to those school and AAU meets, to the smell of chlorine, to crowding around the results lists to find my name. Sometimes I wish I'd had the courage, the drive....the vision to continue.

I love the Olympic commercials, but the one in the last Summer Olympics really hit me.

Luck doesn't get you to the Olympic Games
You can't wish yourself onto the podium
You can't buy it or hope for it
It's not enough to dream about it
Luck didn't get me to London
I swam here

Anything worth achieving—like an Olympic medal, or publication, is not about luck. You can't sit on the sidelines and wish it to happen. You can't dream your way to the best-seller list.

Writing takes hard work. It takes study and teach-ability and coaching and rewriting…and more rewriting…and more rewriting. You only get published if you don't quit.

Dive in. Keep Writing. Stay True to the Journey. And don't stop Believing.

This has been a message from your My Book Therapy coach.

Now Go, and Write Something Brilliant!

Susie May

Did you like this book? Thank you for reading!

I love to help authors with their craft, encouraging them and equipping them with tools to get published and stay published. I do hope you enjoyed our "conversations" and that they helped you as you grew your story.

If you're interested in more resources on writing craft, or even growing your career as a novelist, check out our website: www.my-booktherapy.com. Sign up to receive the daily dose of writing craft, and check out our programs and/or events. We have something for everyone!

If this book clicked with you, I'd be ever so grateful if you'd share that with me (susan@mybooktherapy.com) and others by way of a review on Amazon.com.

Go—write something brilliant!

Would you like a free infographic and 1-hour lesson on how to build a powerful character?

Check out our Story Equation Mini-Course!
(http://novel.academy/courses/TheSEQ/)

About the Author

Susan May Warren

is the RITA award-winning, best-selling author of over fifty novels. With over a million books sold, Susan has won the Christy award twice, and been a finalist eight times. She is also a multi-time winner of the Inspirational Reader's Choice contest and the ACFW Carol Award. She specializes in characterization and has won acclaim for her gripping stories and suspenseful plots. Susan teaches on writing at conferences around the nation and is the founder of www.MyBookTherapy.com, www.LearnHowToWriteANovel.com, and Novel.Academy, all resources for helping aspiring writers.

More writing resources by Susan May Warren

How to Write a Brilliant Novel

Have you always wanted to write a novel but didn't know where to start? This book is for you. With proven techniques, easy to understand explanations, and practical steps, *How to Write a Brilliant Novel* will teach you how a story is structured and then take you through the process of creating and marketing your novel.

Topics include:

- How to HOOK your reader,

- Elements and flow of scenes,

- How to build storyworld,

- Secrets to sizzling dialogue,

- Proven self-editing techniques,

- Synopsis and query letter writing,

- How to manage your writing career—and everything in between!

How to
Write a
Brilliant
Romance

MY BOOK THERAPY

CBA Best-selling,
RITA & Christy award-winning novelist
and writing coach

Susan May Warren

Why do fools fall in love?
The easy, step-by-step method of crafting a powerful romance

How to Write a Brilliant Romance

The easy, step-by-step method of crafting a powerful performance

What does it take to write a brilliant romance? Susan May Warren knows exactly how - and you're about to find out.

Now, for the first time, she's revealing her step-by-step romance writing steps that will show you how to craft an award-winning romance.

Secrets like:

- How do I structure my romance?
- How do I create likable heroes and heroines?
- How should my hero and heroine meet?
- How do I make two characters fall in love?
- How do I write a sizzling kiss?
- How do I create believable conflict?
- How do I keep tension high in the middle of my story?
- How do I put romance on every page?
- What is the breakup and why do I need it?
- Most importantly, how do I create a unique romance that touches the heart of my reader?

Find the answers to these questions as well as a few secrets to creating award-winning romances.

With ten ingredients and step-by-step instructions you'll learn how to plot and write a powerful, layered romance designed to win readers. Susan May Warren has coached hundreds of writers into publication, onto best-seller lists, and onto the awards platforms. (And she lives what she teaches. Susan is a best-selling author of over 50 novels, has won the Rita, the Christ, and the Carol.)

Advanced Brilliant Writing

An amazing novel has two elements - deep characterization of a sympathetic hero, and a compelling, wide, breathtaking plot. But how do you create deep characters and wide plots and then apply them to your story. It's time to learn Advanced (Brilliant) Writing. The follow-up to *How to Write a Brilliant Novel*, the workbook utilizes RITA and Christy award-winning best-selling novelist Susan May Warren's easy to apply explanations, exercises, and intuitive methods to teach you in-depth techniques that will turn any novel from boring. . . to brilliant.

You'll learn:

- How to plot a profound character change journey
- An easy technique to reveal backstory to your readers
- How to weave emotion into your scene for the most impact
- How to keep tension high through the use of stakes and motivations
- A unique plotting trick to widen your plot
- Techniques to how to make your hero. . . heroic
- The difference between subplots and layers
- A powerful use for secondary characters
- How the perfect villain can help you plot your story

. . . and much more, including the scene that every book MUST have!

"If you're intending to write a best-selling novel, I can think of no better place to start than Susan May Warren's *Advance Brilliant Writing*. This is a book for those who need to dig into the techniques of writing—not just hear the happy-talk, big picture stuff that is so often heard at conferences. If you really want to get into the nuts and bolts of writing strong fiction, then this is for you. Clear practical advice from an award-winning novelist." *Chip MacGregor, Literary Agent, MacGregory Literary*

My Brilliant Book Buddy

The writing journey can be long and lonely. It's easy to get lost in the weeds of your story, not sure where you are headed. . . or why. Wouldn't it be nice to have a guide along the way? Someone to point you in the right direction, and keep you focused on the next story step?

A manuscript companion to the foundational writer's workbooks *How to Write a Brilliant Novel* and *Advanced Brilliant Writing*, My Brilliant Book Buddy puts feet to all the steps needed to create a powerful book, guiding you through character creation, plotting the inner and outer journey, creating essential scenes, and word-painting. With step-by-step instruction, it helps you craft the perfect Black Moment, and pushes you all the way to the Climactic Ending.

"The Book Buddy is my new best friend! It takes all of the helpful tools, charts, and tips from her workbooks and puts them in one place. It's like having Susan May Warren in the room helping you craft your story! I can't recommend it highly enough!" *Melissa Tagg, multi-published romance author*